Mind Mapping Made Easy
for family historians

Transform your genealogy research with this practical illustrated step-by-step guide

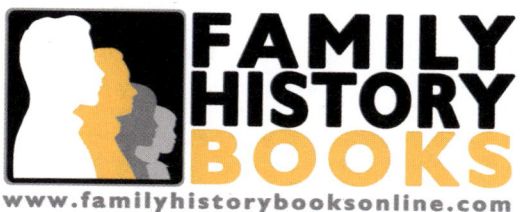

www.familyhistorybooksonline.com

MIND MAPPING MADE EASY FOR FAMILY HISTORIANS

Transform Your Genealogy Research with this practical illustrated step-by-step guide

Published by

Family History Books
the publishing imprint of the Family History Federation
a registered charity number 1038721
P.O. Box 62 Sheringham,
Norfolk NR26 9AR

ISBN: 978-1-916599-04-8

First published 2024

Copyright © Linda Hammond and Family History Books 2024

Family History Books is the trading name of the
Federation of Family History Societies (Services) Ltd

All rights reserved. No part of this book may be reproduced, or stored in a retrieval system or transmitted in any form or by any means, electronic, mechanical, photocopying, recording or otherwise, without the prior approval of the Family History Federation.

Linda Hammond MSc has asserted her rights to be identified as the author of her original work.

by Linda Hammond

CONTENTS

	Introduction	1
Chapter 1	What is a mind map?	3
Chapter 2	How do I start?	6
Chapter 3	Why mind mapping works	11
Chapter 4	Why use mind maps for genealogy?	13
Chapter 5	How to use mind maps for genealogy	15
Chapter 6	Specific uses of mind maps in genealogy	17
Chapter 7	Mind-mapping concepts	18
Chapter 8	Examples illustrating the versatility of mind maps	22
Chapter 9	Mind-mapping software	57
	Conclusion	72
List of illustrations		73
Bibliography and further reading		74

INTRODUCTION

This book is suitable for anyone wanting to improve their family history research skills by employing the use of mind maps. If you are a complete beginner to mind maps, fear not; this book will guide you every step of the way.

If you already have some experience of working with mind maps and are just looking for inspiration, this book will give you plenty of ideas. So, join me as we unlock the potential of mind maps as a powerful tool in your genealogical journey.

Mind maps are certainly not a recent invention. The British psychologist, Tony Buzan, introduced the term "mind mapping" in the 1970s. He popularised the concept, but the technique itself is not new and has been used by many philosophers and great thinkers throughout history since the third century. The earliest known example of a mind map is the *Tree of Porphyry*, created by the Greek philosopher Porphyry of Tyre around AD300.

CHAPTER 1

WHAT IS A MIND MAP?

For those of you who are unfamiliar with mind maps and are encountering them for the first time, here is an example of the type of mind maps we are going to create.

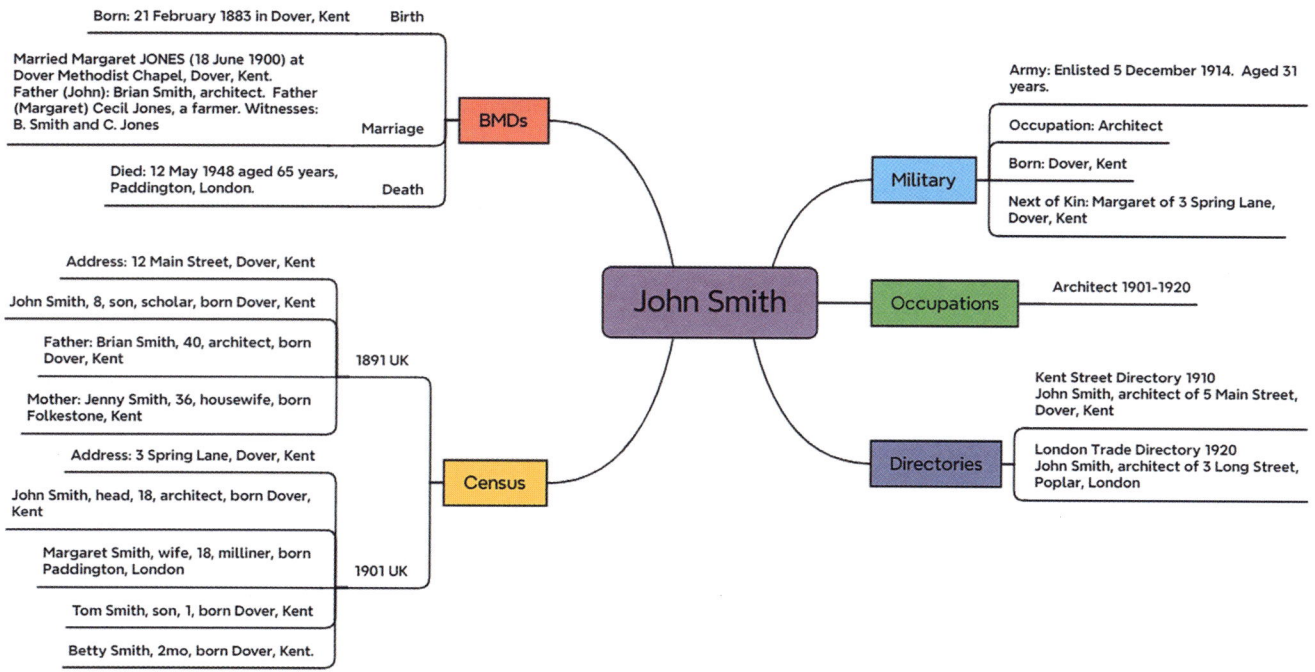

John Smith Mind Map

I have specifically used a genealogy-related mind map, as this is the subject area we will exploring.

Personally, I learned about mind maps when I first started work as a teacher in a large primary school, and it was in that capacity that I began exploring the use of mind maps. Discovering their potential for learning and the profound effect they can have on our comprehension of a topic motivated me to use them, both for myself and with my students, throughout my career.

Children, in particular, love mind maps! Mind maps are a fun, visual way to organise your thoughts and ideas. They are also simple to use, easy to draw and can be created quickly. Mind maps help you stay focussed as you delve deeper into a topic. With mind maps in your armoury you can effortlessly assimilate information, ensuring that you can recall it when the need arises. In fact, the enduring appeal of mind maps lies in their ability to tap into the natural way our brains process information. By using visual connections, mind maps mirror the way our thoughts link together, making it easier to understand and remember information.

Allow me to illustrate this with an example unrelated to family history, but one we will all I'm sure be familiar with.

Picture yourself back at school, sitting in your grammar class. The teacher is droning on about the eight different parts of speech in the English language. You are copying down notes furiously, trying to remember all the definitions and rules. It's not exactly the most exciting experience, but I bet many of you can recall doing exactly that during your own school days!

You would most likely end up with a couple of pages like this:

THE EIGHT PARTS OF SPEECH

There are eight parts of speech in the English language: noun, pronoun, verb, adjective, adverb, preposition, conjunction and interjection.

1. NOUN
A noun is the name of a person, place, thing, quality or idea.
e.g. Robert, Emily, London, China, table, cat, honesty, love, happiness.

2. PRONOUN
A pronoun is a word which replaces a noun.
We have subject pronouns: e.g. I, you, he/she/it, we and they.
And object pronouns: e.g. me, you, him/her, us and them.

3. VERB
A verb expresses action or state.
e.g. singing, belongs, looks.

4. ADJECTIVE
An adjective describes a noun.
e.g. handsome, green, ugly.

5. ADVERB
An adverb describes a verb.
e.g. quickly, nicely, fluently.

6. PREPOSITION
A preposition shows a relationship between things.
There are 3 types of preposition.
Time: e.g. in, on, at.
Place; e.g. in, on, at.
Direction: e.g. into, towards, trough.

7. CONJUNCTION
A conjunction joins words or clauses.
Single-word: e.g. because, yet, and.
Compound word: e.g. as long as, in order to, even if.

8. INTERJECTION
An interjection is a word used to express emotion.
e.g. Wow! Ouch! Huh!

The eight parts of speech table

Certainly, this contains all the information that you need to learn about the eight parts of speech, but it's not very user-friendly. It's very wordy, visually unappealing and decidedly uninspiring. It doesn't make you want to learn the subject, and there's no way you would find it easy to memorise this information in its current format.

This is where mind maps come into their own. A mind map can effortlessly transform the same rather dull information into a clear and interesting format. I have chosen to draw this mind map by hand, just to illustrate that even if you choose not to use any mind-mapping software, the process still works.

No more tedious pages of black and white notes. Welcome to the world of colourful and captivating mind maps which reveal everything at a glance. All that information is now easily accessible. The layout and use of colour not only help our brain absorb the information, but also to remember it, making it easier to recall when we need it.

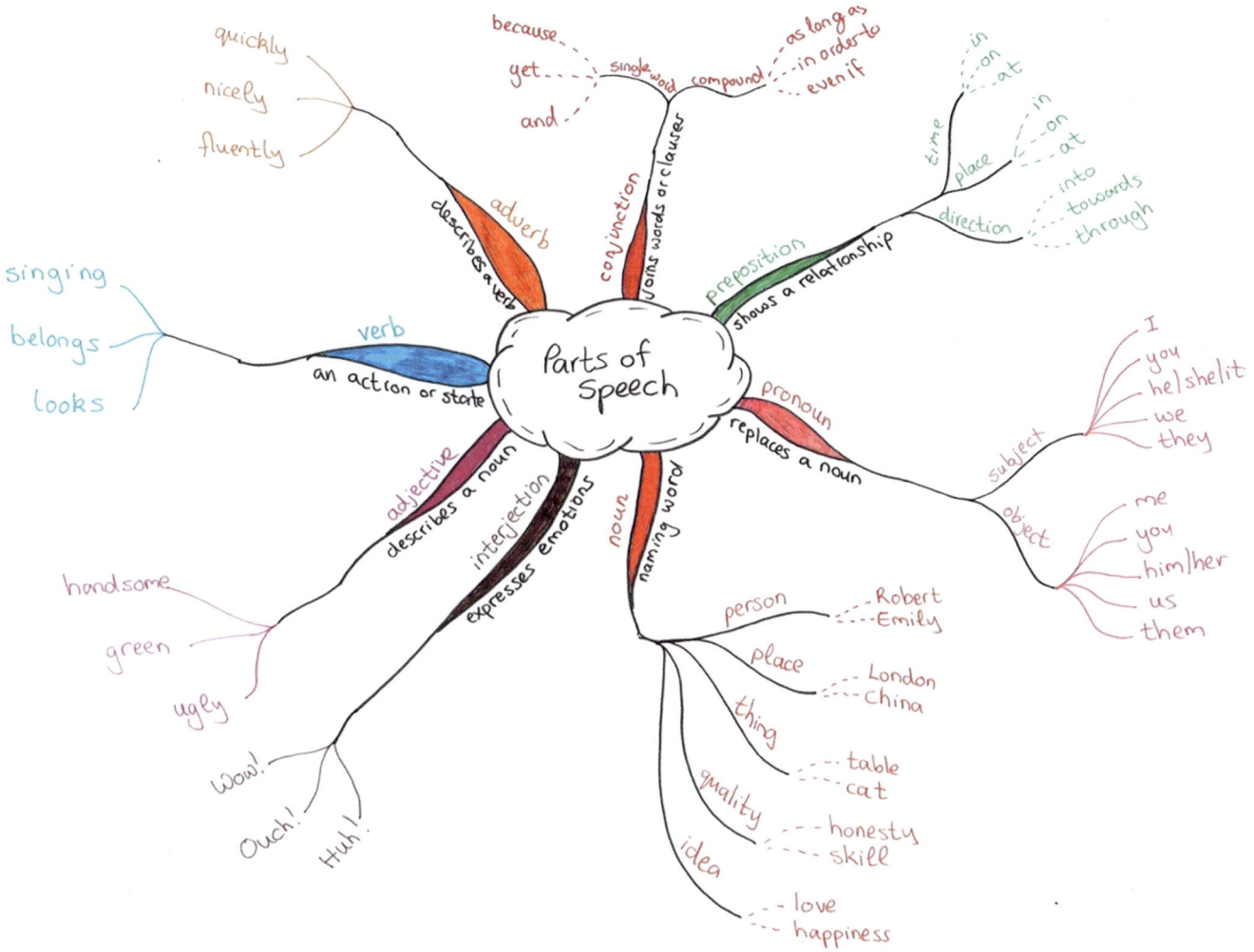

The eight parts of speech mind map

Even if you have never used a mind map before, I hope that this book will convince you to embrace the concept. Whether you prefer to create your mind maps with pen and paper, or use a mind-mapping software package, you will find them invaluable in every stage of your family history research.

CHAPTER 2

HOW DO I START?

We have seen what a mind map looks like, but how do you actually draw one, and what is the idea behind it?

Let me introduce you again to our fictional John Smith, whom we saw in our first sample mind map.

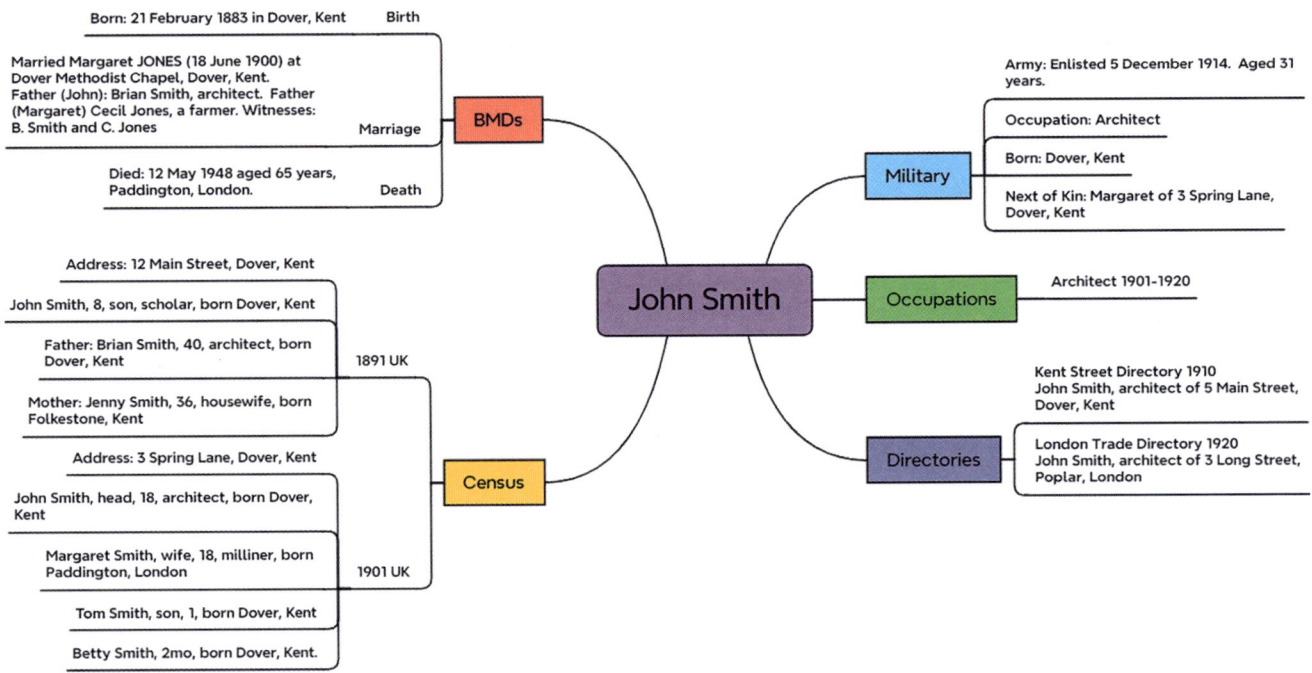

This is a very simple mind map chosen to illustrate how to construct a mind map and demonstrate how they work.

Now, let's go back to the beginning and look at the actual process of constructing this particular mind map. The technique is the same, regardless of whether you are drawing the mind map by hand, with pen and paper, or using a computer software package.

Imagine you are researching our fictional John Smith and you want to create a mind map which will enable you to visualise and organise all the information you have gathered on him in a clear and coherent manner.

The main theme of this mind map is "John Smith". The central topic will therefore be labelled "John Smith". You would draw the first box with his name written in it, and put this in the centre of your page.

In mind-mapping terminology this is called a node. This main central node is from where everything stems; it is the central idea or subject of your mind map.

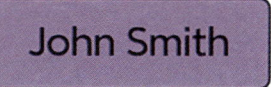

From the main node you then go on to create separate sub-nodes for each subject area. The next topic might be, for example, birth, marriage and death information. So, you could then create a branch to the sub-node, labelled BMDs. You will notice the title has been kept short. We will go into the reasons for this later, but the golden rule is to keep the text as concise as possible.

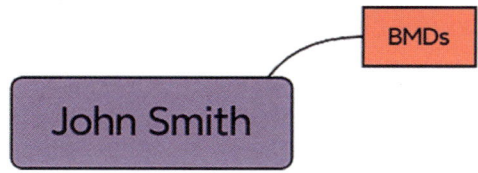

Next you add additional branches or, as they are sometimes termed, twigs or sub-branches, to the BMDs node to identify each area of BMDs. So, in this case birth, marriage and death.

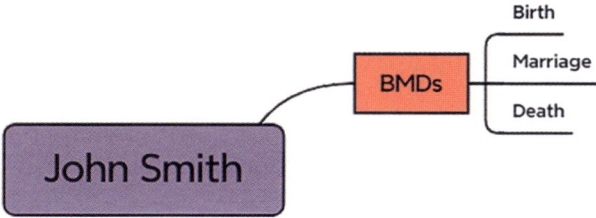

Finally, you add branches to each of these nodes to show all the information you have gleaned in your research so far on John Smith pertaining to each subject area.

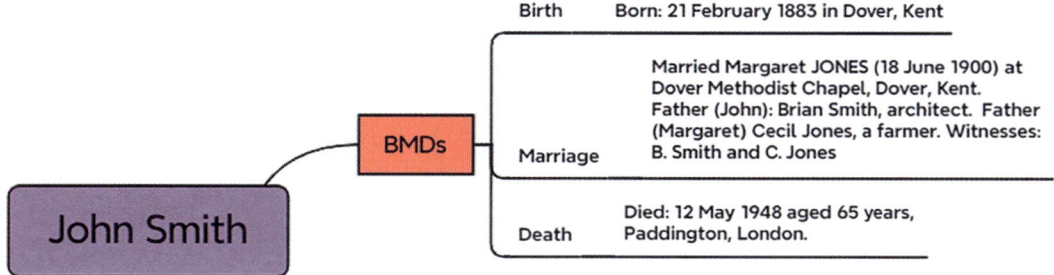

You continue in the same way with each area of your research.

We will now add in any census data.

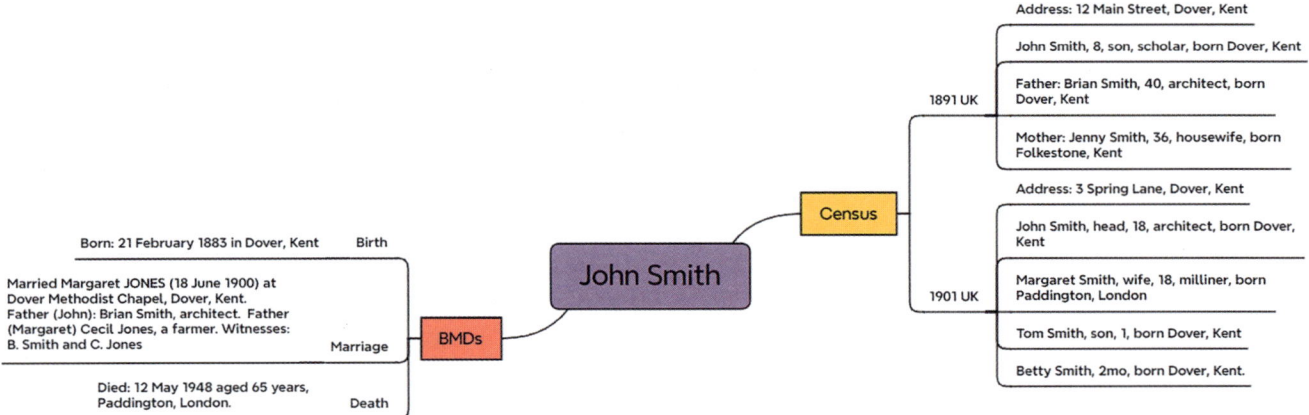

You will notice that the BMDs node has now moved to the other side of the central topic node. If you are using a software package, as you add branches and nodes, the program may automatically reorganise the layout so that everything is clear to see.

However, you can still change the position of these nodes should you wish to do so. Obviously if you are creating your mind map with pen and paper, you will find it more difficult to reorganise your sub-nodes as you progress without resorting to rubbing them out and redrawing them. This is one of the limitations of hand-drawn mind maps.

Next, we can add in John's military career details, including any information obtained from his enlistment record.

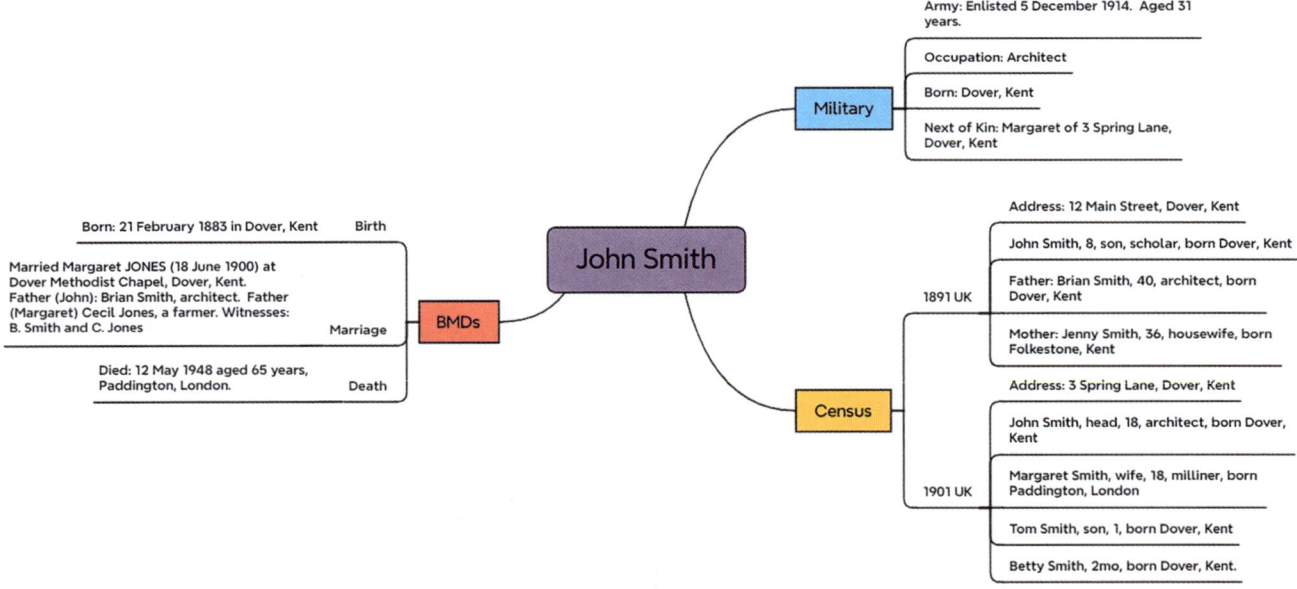

Then we can add his occupations and the applicable dates.

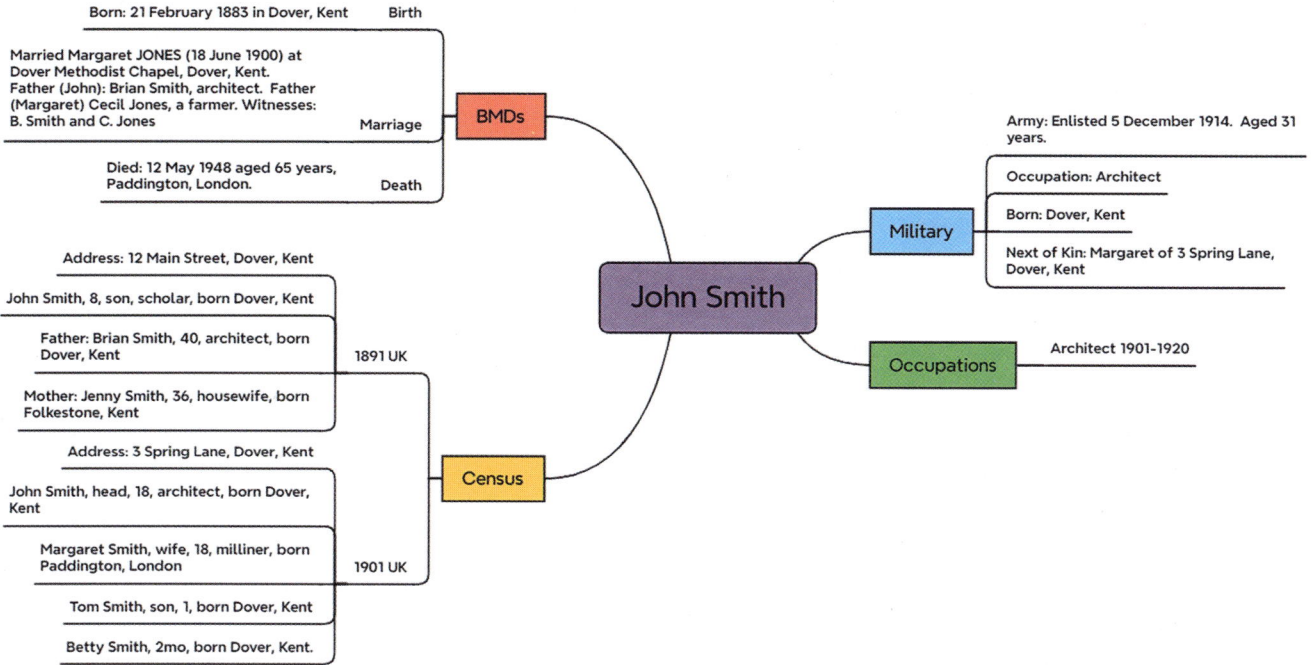

And finally, entries from street and trade directories can be incorporated to complete our mind map.

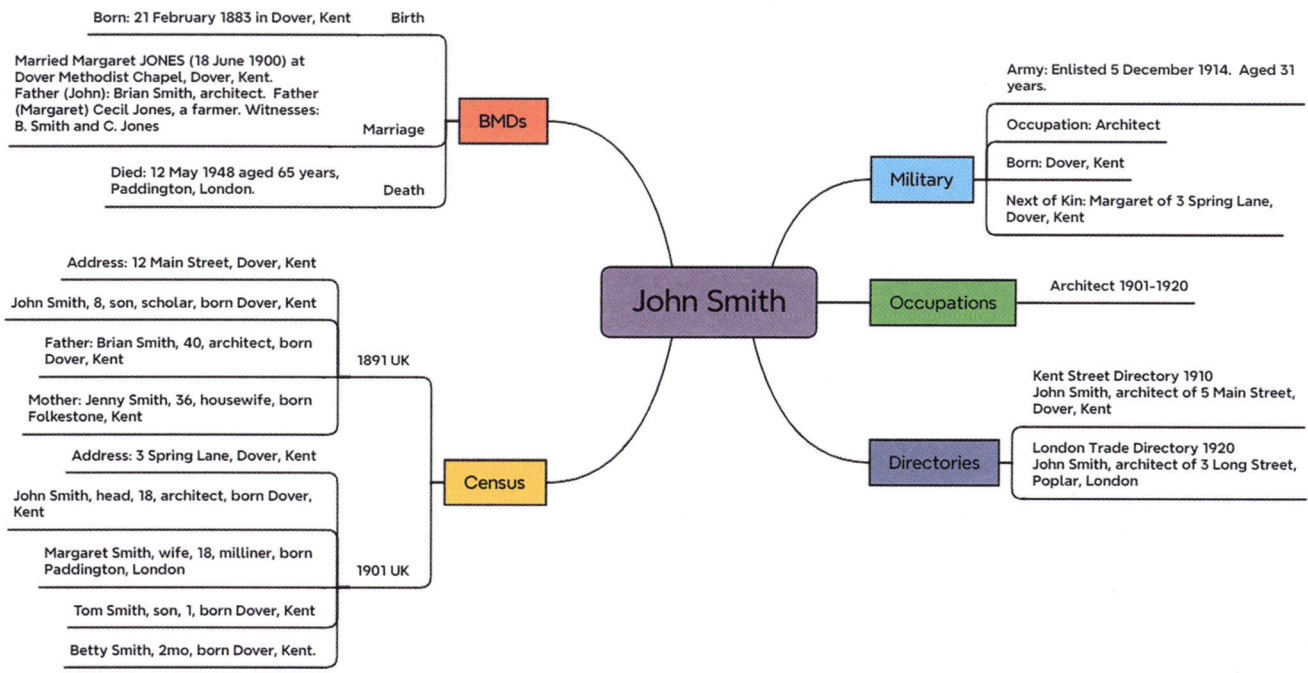

Colour has been used creating this simple mind map, just to help each node stand out. Later we will discuss further uses for colour when constructing your mind maps which can enhance their effectiveness and make them more user-friendly.

Now you might be thinking that all this information is already held in your regular family history software package on your computer. So why bother with a mind map?

However, consider the challenge of locating and analysing all that information from your records in one go. Navigating through different pages and levels within the software package can be time-consuming. Even if you print it out, you will end up with pages of text or family group sheets, making it difficult to see everything together in a cohesive way; and printing out a family tree doesn't guarantee you have all the information on that person – in fact it generally only shows the minimal information on any one person.

On the other hand, a mind map provides a visual representation of *all* the data that makes it easy to access and simple to analyse and make connections.

If you are still not convinced that the mind map can give you quicker and easier access to your research, try this simple test. Look back at the full John Smith mind map on page 9 and answer these simple questions:

1. When and where was John born?
2. Where did he live shortly after his marriage?
3. How long was he there for?
4. When did John join the army?

Hopefully you can see how easy it is to access and analyse all that information. Whether you are searching for gaps in your research or trying to break down a brick wall, this mind map allows you to view all the data in one place with clarity.

CHAPTER 3

WHY MIND MAPPING WORKS

We're now going to briefly look at why mind mapping works, and how mind maps can help us with our genealogical research. As genealogists, we embark on a journey of discovery, tracing our family's roots and unravelling the intricate tapestry of our ancestral heritage. This requires organisation, creativity, and a knack for connecting the dots between seemingly disparate pieces of information. Mind mapping is an invaluable tool that allows us to navigate our way through our genealogy research with ease and effectiveness.

The human mind is naturally drawn to visual stimuli. Mind maps tap into this innate capacity, using a graphical representation to organise and structure information in a way that is both visually appealing and intellectually stimulating. By visually representing relationships and connections, mind maps allow us to understand complex concepts; this is what makes them ideal tools for genealogy research. You can even incorporate colour coding, symbols, and images to enhance the visual impact of your mind maps.

Mind maps help you to visualise connections, identify problems and enable you to plan your work easily. They convey information in a simple visual format which enables users to analyse and work with the data quickly and efficiently.

John Medina, the American neurobiologist, said, *We are incredibly good at recording images. If you hear some information, then three days later you will remember only ten per cent of it. If you add a picture to it, then sixty-five per cent will be retrievable.* In his book *Brain Rules,* he explains that the more visual the information is, the more easily we can absorb and retain it.

And this is what we want to achieve. We don't want to trawl through pages of notes to find information; we want it to be quick and easy. Once we have the information, we want to be able to find the relevant data, work with it and use it. And once we've started working on a dilemma or a brainstorm, we want to retain that information and absorb it, to enable us to complete the task simply and quickly. Mind maps can help us do all this.

Mind maps are not mere lists or outlines; they are catalysts for creativity. As genealogists, we often encounter brick walls and dead ends in our research. Mind maps provide a platform for brainstorming potential solutions, identifying overlooked leads, and overcoming challenges.

As we have seen, a well-written mind map is so much easier to read and absorb than a page of notes. It can give you a clear understanding of a concept and allow you to gain an insight into the bigger picture of your project. It can also act as a quick reference tool and can increase your ability to memorise and internalise the topic – something which is always useful when you're trying to recall facts.

Unravelling the intricacies of a family tree can be a daunting task. Mind maps offer a clear and structured framework for organising genealogical data, making it effortless to navigate and analyse vast amounts of information. By creating mind maps for individual ancestors, families, or specific topics, genealogists can easily identify patterns, relationships, and gaps in their research.

Mind mapping is an invaluable tool that can transform your genealogical research. It gives you the power to organise information, stimulate creativity, and track your progress. You can start by creating mind maps for key family branches, research projects, or specific questions you want to answer. You can also share your mind maps with fellow family historians to spark discussions and inspire new ideas.

The fact that mind maps are so flexible also means they can be used in all aspects of your research and for a variety of situations. Admittedly, creating effective mind maps requires practice and while there are no rigid rules, there are guidelines and techniques that can be employed to get the best from your mind map. This book aims to be your comprehensive guide to exploring and mastering mind maps. Their only limitation is your imagination!

CHAPTER 4

WHY USE MIND MAPS FOR GENEALOGY?

Having looked at what a mind map is and why they work, now let's look at how they help with our genealogical research – and specifically why.

I would imagine that many of you reading this book use family history software packages to store and organise your genealogical data. Whether you have purchased a software package or rely on the online storage provided by platforms such as Ancestry or FindMyPast, these tools can help you maintain your research and safeguard it.

Those seeking a more traditional approach may have chosen to preserve their genealogical records, including comprehensive family group sheets and photocopies of pertinent documents, in physical filing systems. This traditional method ensures that genealogical data remains readily accessible for review and updating as fresh information or evidence emerges.

Printing out family trees is a common practice among genealogists; it provides a tangible representation of your research progress. It also helps clarify who you need to look for next, or identify where the gaps are in your trees. All family history software packages and online platforms allow you to do this, some with a variety of display options. While family trees are great for displaying genealogical data, they are, however, less effective for analysing it.

Family history software packages also can't help you sort out and store all those odds and ends of data which don't fit neatly into a specific category. Think of all those scraps of paper and sticky notes you have attached inside folders or around your computer screen. While you may have no idea where they belong, you know that they will eventually fit somewhere some day!

Who can empathise with this image? We do our best to stay organised, but with the best will in the world, it's not always easy.

Mind maps, on the other hand, can cope with all these things and more. As well as helping plan our research, identifying gaps and organising our thoughts, they can also show information more clearly and allow you to see immediately what needs to be done next.

Mind maps are not intended to replace traditional genealogical software. Rather, they complement these tools, offering a unique perspective on your research data. Genealogy software excels at storing and managing structured data, while mind maps excel at visualising and analysing complex relationships. By utilising both tools effectively, you can gain a comprehensive understanding of your family's history.

Mind maps are great when your brain is in overload with too much information and chaos is reigning! They help you to "declutter" your brain and then you can see the bigger picture more easily and start linking things together and gaining structure. If you have everything as a list or report, you have to go back and read through it all to find what you're looking for. A mind map allows you to explore a person's life, get an in-depth look at a document or plan your next steps, whilst internalising the information simply and quickly.

Imagine you're tracing your family's roots back to the nineteenth century, or maybe even earlier. You've amassed a wealth of genealogical data, including family trees, source citations, and historical records. However, as your research expands, it becomes increasingly challenging to manage and analyse this amount of information. This is where mind maps come into play, offering a powerful visual representation to organise and structure your data.

Let's consider a specific example. You've uncovered a historical document that mentions a supposed distant relative, but the document lacks enough information to identify their exact connection to your family tree. A traditional family tree may not provide the clarity you need to make the connection and traditional family history software does not really allow you to even enter the person. However, a mind map can effectively visualise the relationships between individuals and historical records, allowing you to identify patterns and connections that might otherwise go unnoticed.

By creating a mind map centred on the historical document, you can visually represent the individuals mentioned in the document, their relationships to each other and their potential links to your family tree. This visual representation can help you uncover hidden connections and identify potential ways forward in your research. Later in chapter eight we will look at this type of use for a mind map and how it can help with your research.

CHAPTER 5

HOW TO USE MIND MAPS FOR GENEALOGY

Mind maps are very flexible and can be used at various stages of your genealogical research. In this chapter, we shall explore the different ways you can use them throughout the research process, whether it is the planning stage, collating information, breaking down brick walls, identifying gaps in your research, analysing data or presenting your results. Mind maps will prove to be an invaluable ally throughout your complete genealogical journey.

Brainstorming

Whatever the problem you are trying to solve, mind mapping can help and also speed up the process. So, whether you are trying to find the connection between two family members, locate specific records in an archive, analyse a genealogical document or resolve a relationship dilemma, mind maps can increase your chances of success.

By keeping all the information in one place, mind maps help you see the whole picture at once. These visual representations of thoughts and ideas have the remarkable capacity to show us pathways that might have otherwise remained hidden. Ultimately, this helps us achieve our goals much more quickly and easily.

Organisation

Mind maps are incredibly versatile tools that help you organise your thoughts and findings. Whether you're trying to locate gaps in your family tree or planning a research trip to a new archive, mind maps are highly effective. They bring together your ideas and observations in a clear and organised way.

Exploring your family history and trying to find missing connections can be tricky, but mind maps help by showing existing links and highlighting gaps visually. They make complex details easy to understand.

When preparing for a research trip to an unfamiliar archive, mind maps help you plan everything step by step; you can map out your research goals, logistics and strategies in a clear way, making the planning process run smoothly.

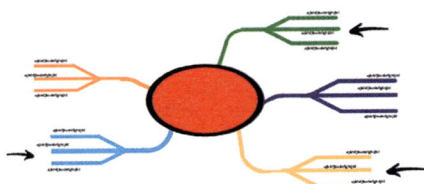

Showing your results

Mind maps go beyond just organising information – they also provide a visual representation of your findings. This simple yet effective method of using a mind map to show your results can yield multiple benefits. Imagine you're attempting to explain a segment of your family tree to a relative or fellow researcher. Utilising a mind map makes this task significantly more straightforward both in terms of explanation and comprehension.

The visual layout of a mind map simplifies the complexities of your findings, making it easier to communicate the information. As a result, the process of sharing and understanding family lines or specific research outcomes becomes notably easier.

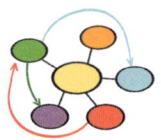

Correlating data

If you are aiming to identify connections between certain family members, a mind map can prove remarkably helpful, more so than a traditional family tree. Consider the scenario where you need to visualise a family's movements within a country or even between different countries. Here too, a mind map will display the evidence clearly and concisely revealing those family migration patterns or relocations with remarkable clarity.

When it comes to piecing together all the details about a person or a subject, the task becomes notably more manageable when you employ a mind map to visually present that information. This approach helps you see the relationships between various pieces of data or evidence, making it easier to grasp the bigger picture and uncover insights that might have otherwise remained hidden. A mind map helps you understand and analyse information more easily by organising facts and ideas in a clear and connected way.

Analysing the evidence

No matter what information you are trying to uncover or understand, a mind map can be your speedy companion. By having all the necessary details laid out in front of you, you can quickly access the information, analyse the evidence and draw conclusions.

Facts and sources can be seamlessly integrated into your mind map. This way, you can thoroughly analyse every aspect of your research, making sure no important piece is overlooked.

CHAPTER 6

SPECIFIC USES OF MIND MAPS IN GENEALOGY

There are many ways you can use mind maps whilst working on your family tree – too numerous to list! This chapter will explore some of the main ways to use mind maps and hopefully inspire you to give them a go.

Specific uses could include:

- planning your research
- analysing a person
- analysing a document
- analysing sources
- finding gaps in your family tree
- breaking down a brick wall
- organising your extended research
- planning a research trip
- carrying out a house history
- constructing a village/local study document
- writing up your family history research.

Basically, as we said before, the only thing limiting your use of mind maps in your genealogical research is your imagination!

Most of these tasks could not be done with a traditional genealogical software package and this is why mind maps are so useful. In chapter eight we will delve into some of these uses in greater depth and explore some detailed examples.

CHAPTER 7

MIND-MAPPING CONCEPTS

We've looked at why mind maps are useful and how they can help us with our research. We've explored their visual appeal and their step-by-step creation process. Now let's delve into the fundamental concepts that underpin mind mapping and why mastering these concepts is crucial if we are to unlock their full potential.

I mentioned earlier that there are no real rules when creating your mind maps. However, there are disciplines which can be good to keep in mind. If you think back to when we constructed that first mind map on John Smith, we discussed concepts such as keeping text short and the use of colour. Now, let me explain why these, and other important concepts, make mind maps so effective

The importance of keeping text short

Let's think about how your brain stores information. Does it store details or information in paragraphs or sentences? Absolutely not! If your brain has to remember text, then short, punchy phrases are the easiest way for it to achieve this. Think how newspaper editors craft attention-grabbing headlines to capture our interest. The shorter and more eye-catching they are, the better. It's important to steer clear of long, lengthy sections of text; the brain just will not be able to take them in and remember them.

Imagine you're trying to remember the information in the following paragraph:

Jack Lynch was born on 20 April 1875 to George and Anne Lynch. They lived in Meadowsweet Cottage in the village of Sandford in Devon. George was a blacksmith in the village. They also had three other children: Lydia who was born the year after Jack, Henry who was born in 1878 and John who was born in 1880. Both boys followed in their father's footsteps and became blacksmiths, whereas Lydia went to work at the nearby manor house as a parlour maid. Jack left Sandford and went to work in London as a carter where he met his wife, Phyllis. Henry and John both stayed in the village. Henry never married, but John married a local girl, Nellie Chatham.

Now look at this information reduced to short bullet points:

- *Parents: George and Anne Lynch (Meadowsweet Cottage, Sandford, Devon)*
- *Children: Jack (20 April 1875), Henry (1878), John (1880) and Lydia (1876)*
- *Jack: Went to London; wife, Phyllis, occupation: carter*
- *Henry: blacksmith, stayed in Sandford and never married*
- *John: blacksmith, stayed in Sandford and married Nellie Chatham*
- *Lydia: parlour maid at Manor House.*

How much easier is that to analyse and remember!

If you are writing a long title on a branch, for example *1891 England census*, then stop and think, and try and break it down into sub-nodes and branches – *census, England, 1891*. That way you can have a node for the census which will have a branch off it to the country. This will then have each census year branching off it. Something like this:

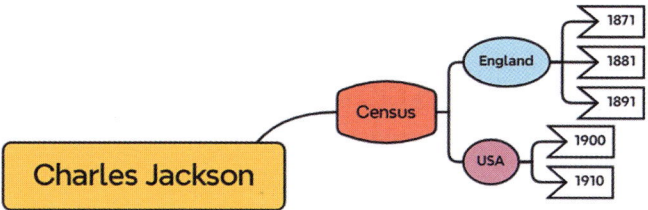

This will ensure that all the information is clearly displayed, well-organised and clear to the reader.

The importance of colour

Adding colour to your mind maps emphatically improves them and makes them more effective. You can use a colour to identify a particular family group, a certain town or a particular record group. Colour coding your mind maps transforms information into a visually captivating chart and breathes life into your research.

Colour is important when creating a mind map and this example clearly illustrates why.

Take a look at this mind map detailing probate and will information for my family. We could have entered this information onto a spreadsheet and it would have been just as clear, but if you then want to organise or rearrange and analyse this information, nothing beats a mind map.

Here is the data as it was collected and put into a simple mind map:

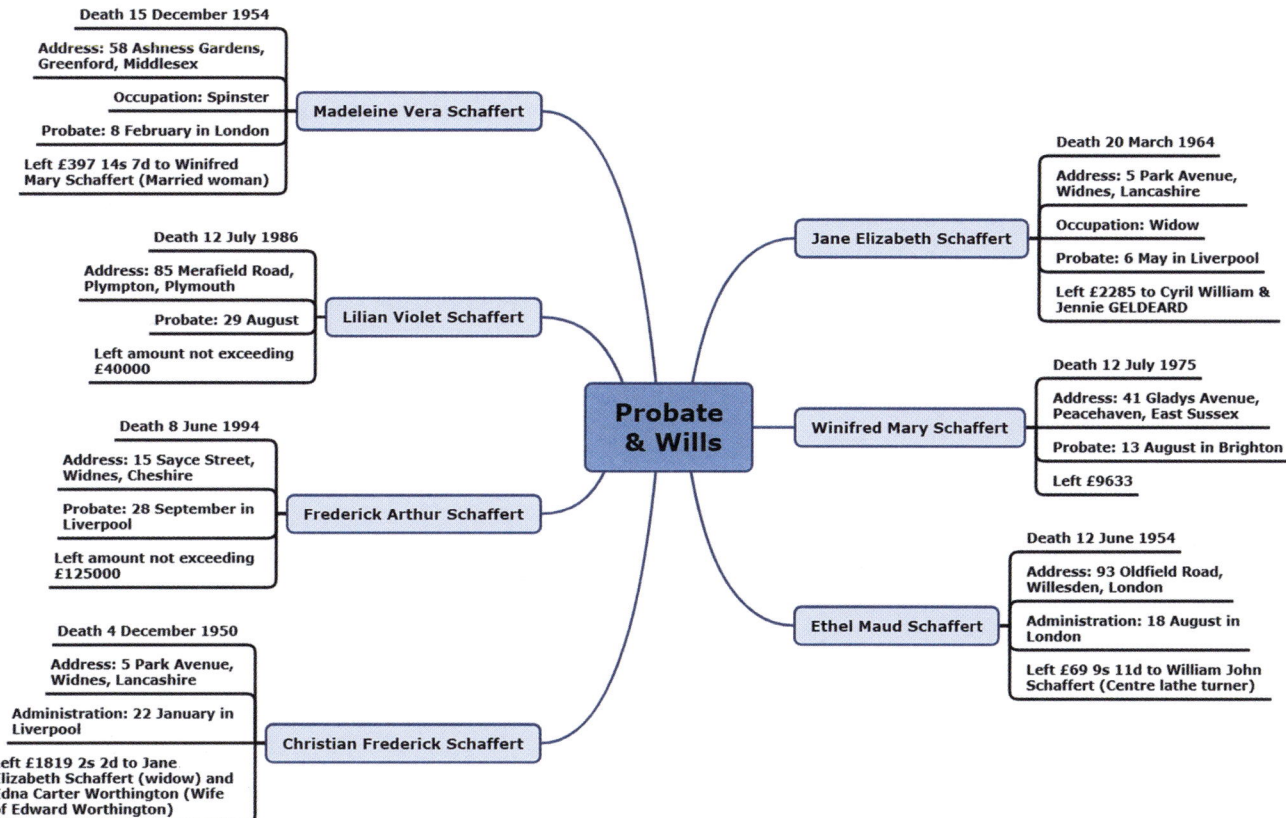

It is clear what we are looking at and the names are obvious, but how are these people connected? Who is related to whom? How many different families are there being researched?

Look what happens when we add colour and sort and rearrange the family groups.

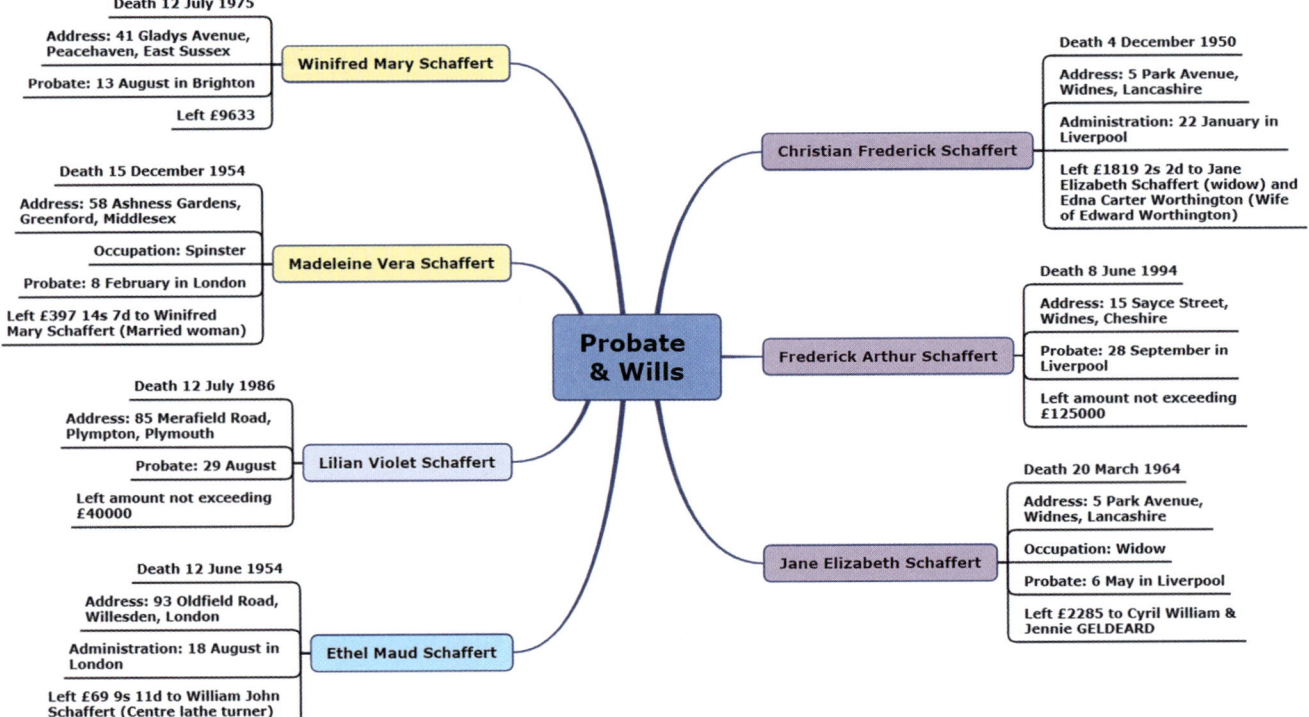

The colour-coded branches leap out at us, showing the family connections instantly. What a difference it makes!

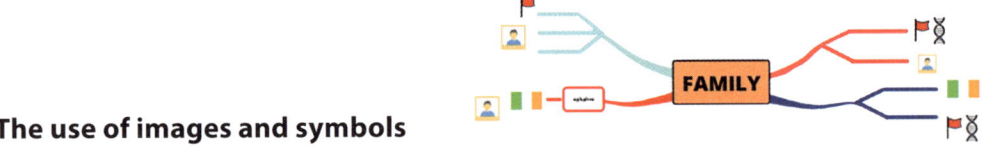

The use of images and symbols

Another useful tool which can help organise your mind maps is to use symbols or images. Most mind-mapping software has its own set of symbols which you can use but you could design your own.

If you were to analyse a particular ancestor, such as my Joseph Richardson here, and wanted to illustrate your findings with colour and symbols, then you could have a basic set to use for birth, marriage and death. You could then incorporate the use of country flags to show where events took place. If you had a photograph of your ancestor you could even incorporate that into the mind map.

This could mean a much more intricate mind map was created like this one.

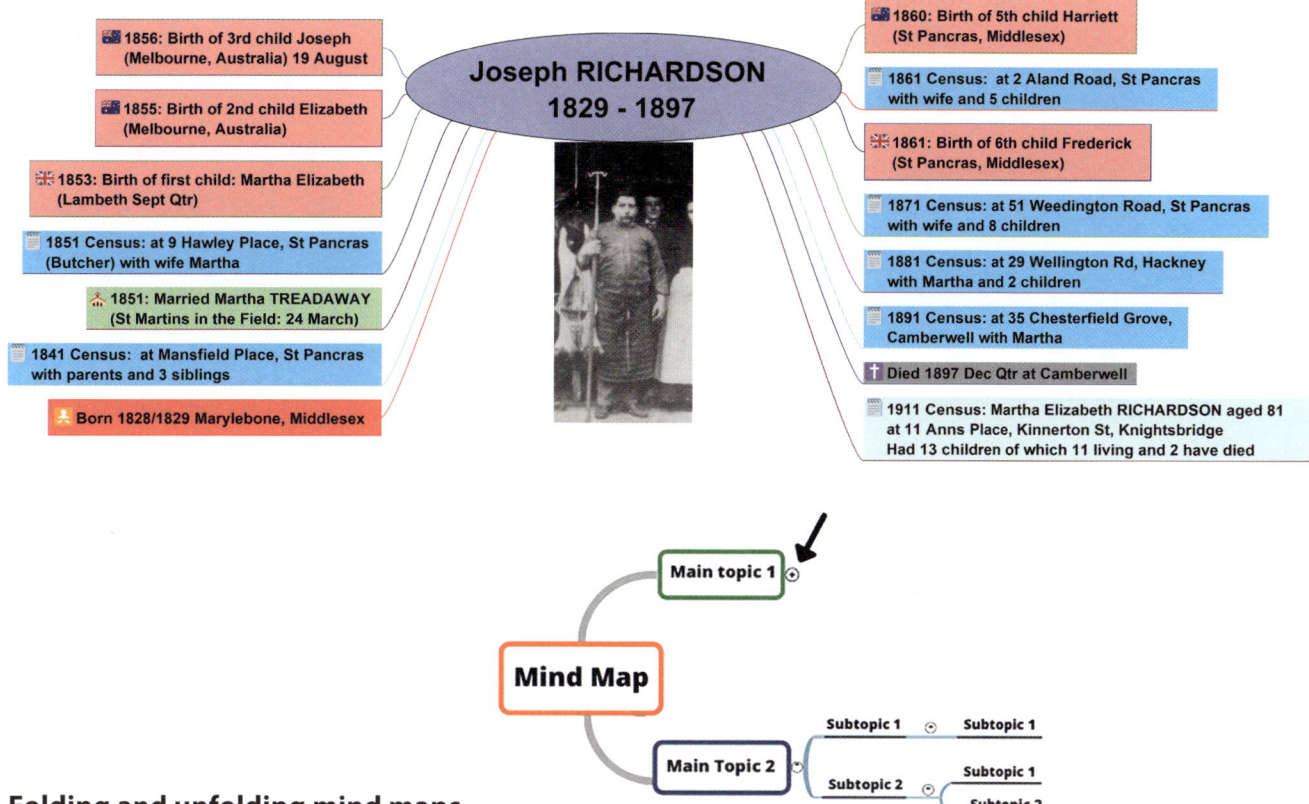

Folding and unfolding mind maps

Another handy feature of mind maps is the collapsible nature of them but this is only possible if you are using a mind-mapping software package. Depending on the package you use, you can control how much information is visible at any given time.

This is especially helpful when working on smaller screens like laptops or tablets; you can limit the information displayed to avoid clutter and optimise the viewing experience. There is a small circle at the end of each node – simply clicking on this allows you to fold and unfold the rest of the information on that branch.

How mind mapping can actually save you time

Some of you might be thinking – *but this will take me ages! I'd rather spend my time researching, not organising all this information into mind maps.* But trust me, in the long run, mind maps will save you time and make your research process smoother and more efficient.

You can add to your mind map at any time, effortlessly drag and drop nodes to rearrange your thoughts, and focus on any section whenever you like. You actually have a flexible and versatile tool always at your fingertips. And the best part is that you can even reuse the same mind map for different research projects by simply copying and pasting branches or even the entire map!

CHAPTER 8

EXAMPLES ILLUSTRATING THE VERSATILITY OF MIND MAPS

In chapter six we explored the various ways you could use mind maps in genealogy. In this chapter we shall take a closer look at some of those concepts.

Planning your research

Mind maps are a great tool for organising your research plans, whether you're looking for records online or in an archive. While it might seem like overkill, using mind maps can help you stay organised throughout your research journey.

Imagine you are researching an ancestor who lived in the Plympton St Mary workhouse in Devon in 1851. You have found them on the census records living in the workhouse in 1851, and these indicate that they were born in Plympton around 1788, before general registration began. You have searched forward to the 1861 census records but cannot find your ancestor.

Now, you need to find any parish or workhouse records that could provide additional insights into your ancestor's life, and can hopefully help you go back to the previous generation of that family.

The local archives for the Plympton area are your best bet for locating these records, but there are also plenty of online websites which will have records or transcriptions of records or even indexes to the records. Doing a general Google search can be worthwhile as you can often find a website devoted to a workhouse or other institution, or a historical site pertaining to it.

I always draw up a mind map of my findings; that way I know I won't forget anything. While a simple list might seem sufficient, a mind map offers a visual and organised approach that will enhance your organisational skills. The expandable nature of a mind map allows you to accommodate additional information at a later point without running out of space. The visual layout of a mind map enables you to see things more clearly and you can keep it to help towards your main research planning.

The mind map I created for this purpose is shown on the next page. It outlines the sources I examined to locate records for the parish of Plympton St Mary and those specifically related to the workhouse or the poor of the parish.

To ensure I didn't miss any potentially relevant records, I compiled the holdings of not only physical archives but also various online websites. Even though some of the website content overlapped, I documented all my findings. This is because even if a website states it holds records from a specific period, there could be gaps in the records that are not reflected on the website's index. Another website might have a different coverage that fills those gaps. Additionally, I didn't differentiate between original scans and transcriptions. The search functions for these types of records can vary; you might find that the original scans are not indexed but the transcriptions are. In such cases, you can use the transcription index to locate the original scan of a record.

MIND-MAPPING MADE EASY FOR FAMILY HISTORIANS

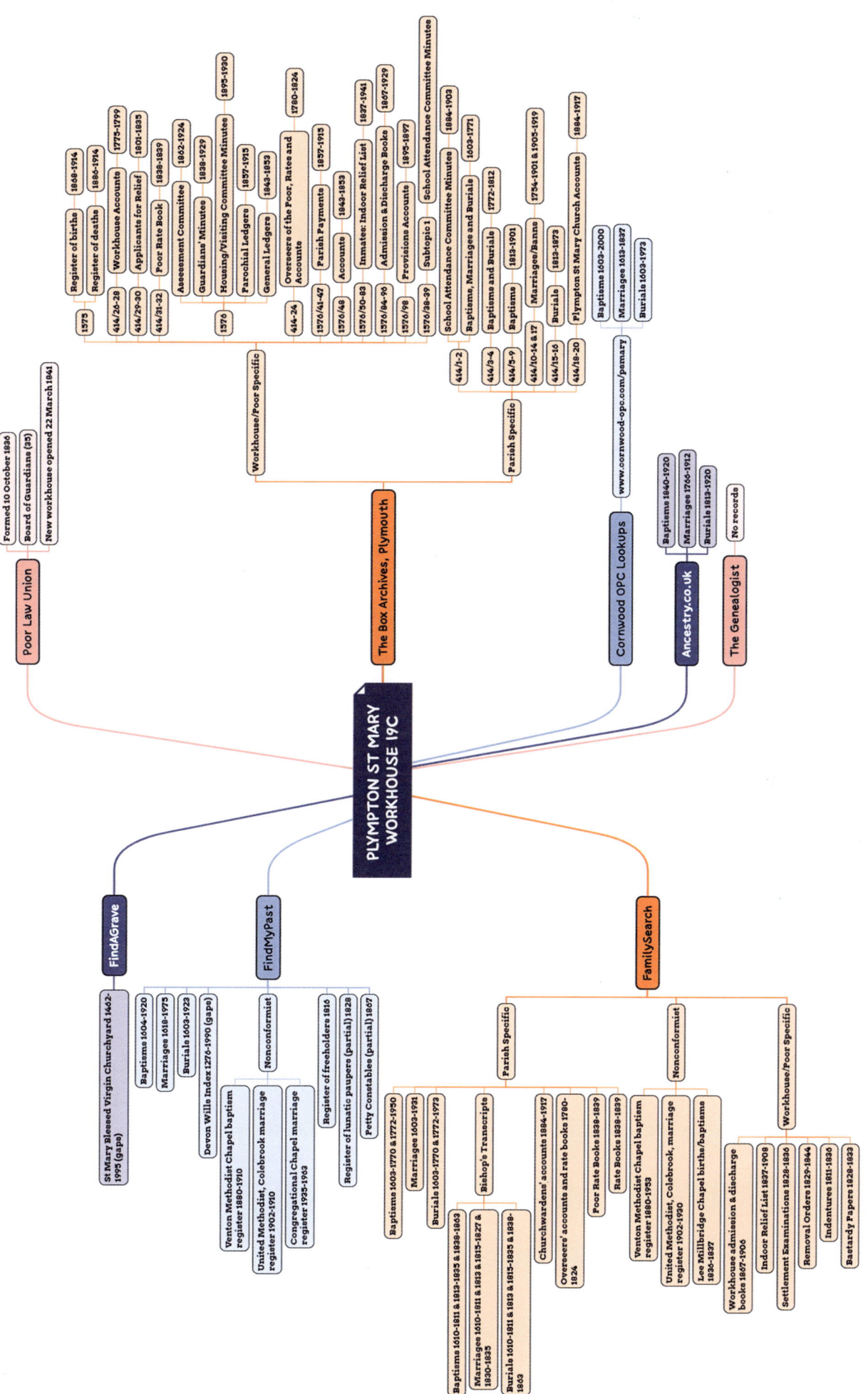

Plympton Workhouse Mind Map

I can now use this mind map to plan my research knowing that I have all the relevant details at my fingertips. I can also use the mind map as a checklist, ticking off records as I locate and check them.

It also means that at a later date if I should find some other relevant records, I can add them to this mind map to complete the analysis. This mind map could then be used to help analyse another ancestor in a similar situation.

Analysing a person

Family history research can often proceed smoothly, but there may be instances where specific individuals or records pose some real challenges. At this point it can be useful to analyse a particular person in greater depth.

I encountered just such an occasion while researching my great-grandfather, Johann Schaffert. He had always been a bit of a stumbling block for me I knew plenty about his life after he had met my great-grandmother Ethel, but his origins were shrouded in mystery.

Obviously, Schaffert was a German name, but German civil records, like those of some other European countries, are organised by administrative districts and there is no centralised national registration index which can be searched. This meant that without knowing the specific town where my ancestor originated, finding his birth records would be an almost impossible task.

As far as I knew I'd never seen mention of any specific town in any of the records I had found for Johann, but I wanted to confirm this, and also to make sure I had gathered every little clue possible to help me with my investigation going back in my research to Germany.

I therefore decided to extract all the information I had on Johann to help confirm this. This process also helped me identify various anomalies like variant spellings of names. Now, I had a comprehensive summary of Johann's life on a single sheet of paper, eliminating the need to sift through pages of notes or screens of information to find specific details.

MIND-MAPPING MADE EASY FOR FAMILY HISTORIANS

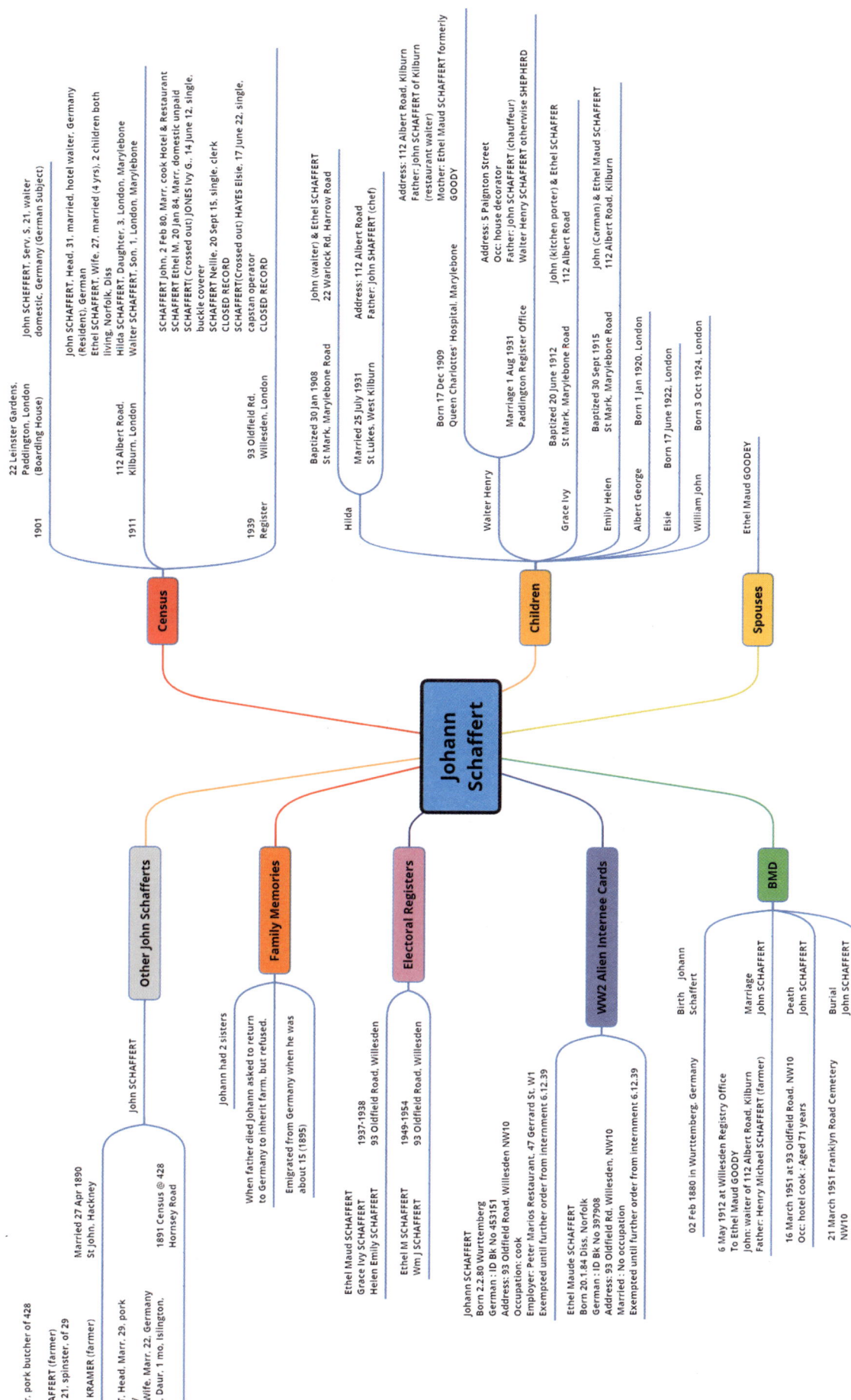

Johann Schaffert Mind Map

Identifying gaps in your research

Whether you keep your family history data stored digitally on software, online, or in physical files, one of the challenges we often encounter is pinpointing those gaps in our research. Family history research relies on work we carried out many months or even years ago and over time we have added new information and built on those same foundations. As each year passes, the world of genealogical research evolves. Archival repositories and the internet have opened up new avenues for exploration, providing greater accessibility to records and sometimes revealing previously inaccessible information.

How regularly do you revisit and review your genealogical research to pinpoint any gaps? It is a good habit to cultivate and one where mind maps can be really beneficial. If these gaps are not addressed, they can become formidable roadblocks in our research – yet we may be completely unaware of their existence due to a lack of thorough analysis.

A frequent stumbling block in our genealogical research can be caused by overlooking some of the children born to a couple. If we only identify some of the children from a marriage, we could be causing ourselves some problems with identifying records for other family members. In the past, it was common practice for aging parents to move in with one of their children, especially if they were widowed or needed assistance. As a result, it's not unusual for a child to be listed as the informant on a parent's death certificate, particularly if they lived together at the same property. If that child is female and has married, thus changing her surname, figuring out who she is becomes a tad more challenging.

This is why knowing all the children who were born to a couple is essential and ensures that we don't overlook any clues that could help us identify family members or events.

There are often clues in our evidence that we have unintentionally missed some family members or made an error:

- a child's birthdate predates their parent's marriage
- a large number of years exists between the marriage date and the birth of the first child
- large gaps between the births of children born to a couple
- children born in close succession, but less than nine months apart
- birthplaces of children differ from those recorded in census records
- failure to identify the death of a child.

Here is an example of a mind map, revisiting our Joseph Richardson whom we met earlier, seeking to identify those exact clues.

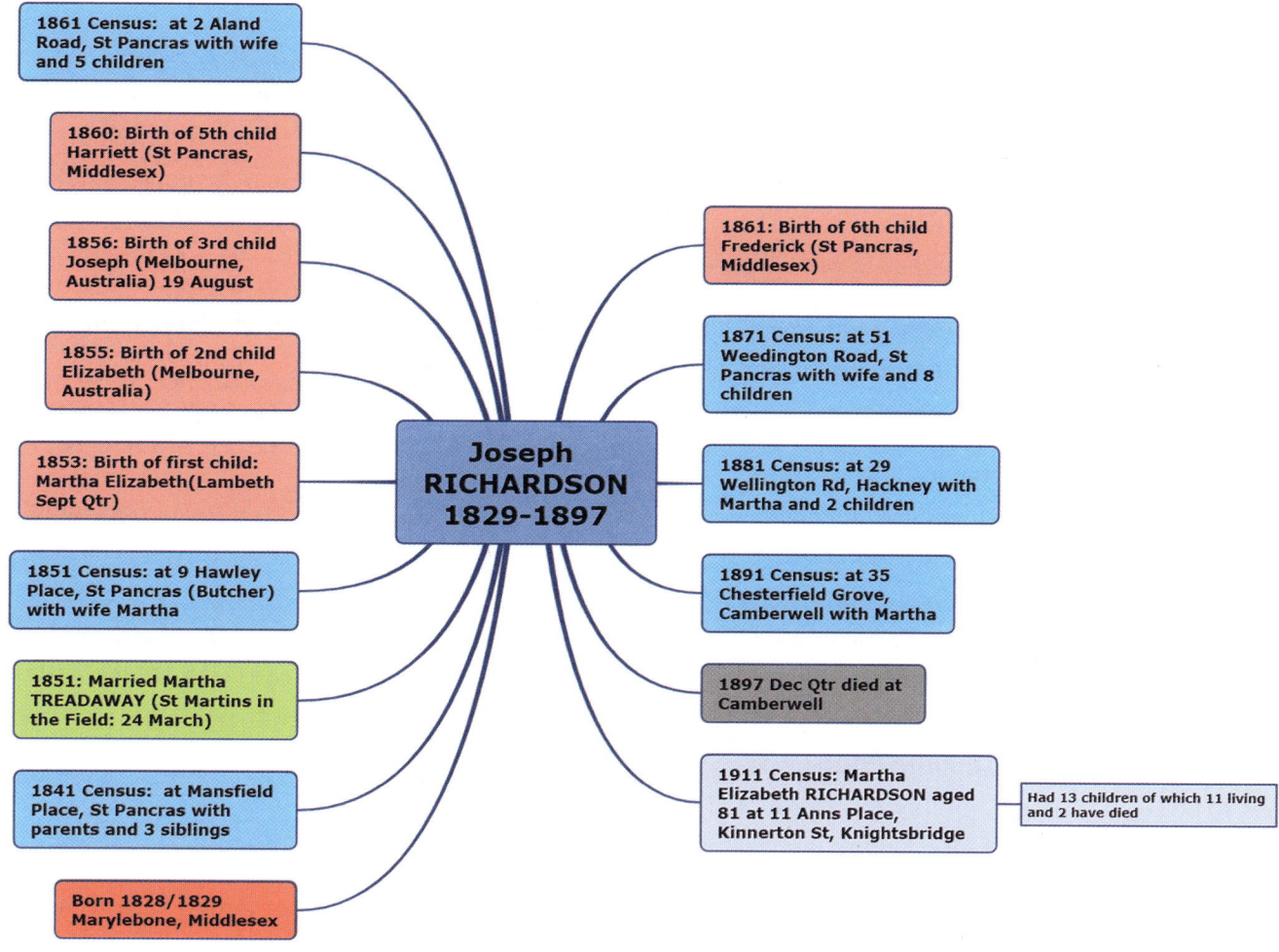

Joseph Richardson Mind Map

We have colour-coded the events to make them easier to identify, but basically this is the life of Joseph Richardson who was born in 1829 and died in 1897. This mind map contains all the details we have, and had we kept this information in our files or software package, and not re-examined it, we may well have overlooked some important details.

All looks good until we get to the 1871 census, which identifies eight children. Frederick, born in 1861, was, we assumed, the couple's sixth child, so we have two missing children. As is usual, in later censuses the number of children dwindles because they leave home or possibly pass away. However, the 1911 census record showing Joseph's widow, Martha, yields even more clues, as she states she has had thirteen children, of which eleven are still living and two have died.

We know of six children born between 1851 and 1861. As the 1871 census shows there are eight children, we know that two of those children were born between 1861 and 1871.

The 1911 census record revealing Martha's total of thirteen children indicates the presence of five additional children born to this couple whose existence we haven't yet unearthed. They may have been born anytime from 1851 to 1897. There are two deceased children but their births could have occurred at any point within the marriage. However, the 1871 census documenting their eight living children implies that even if two children had been born and died prior to this date, three additional offspring still remain to be found, and their births must have occurred between 1871 and 1897.

These are the types of issues which could be so easily overlooked had we not extracted the data into a mind map and analysed it.

Analysing a document

Using a removal order dated 1862, I want to illustrate how a mind map helps you not only analyse a document but plan your next steps.

This order was issued to John Dunn, my great-great-great-grandfather. It is a common surname, Dunn, and the fact that he lived in Bethnal Green, London, meant it has been challenging to locate much information on his family and life.

Having successfully traced John Dunn through the 1851, 1861 and 1871 census returns, I discovered that he died in 1874. Despite some in-depth research, the search for his marriage remains elusive, even though I know their first child, William Richard James Dunn, was born in 1839. The presumption that the couple married prior to this birth is yet to be substantiated. Notably, four additional children were born between 1842 and 1849, adding layers to the intricate puzzle of John Dunn's familial history.

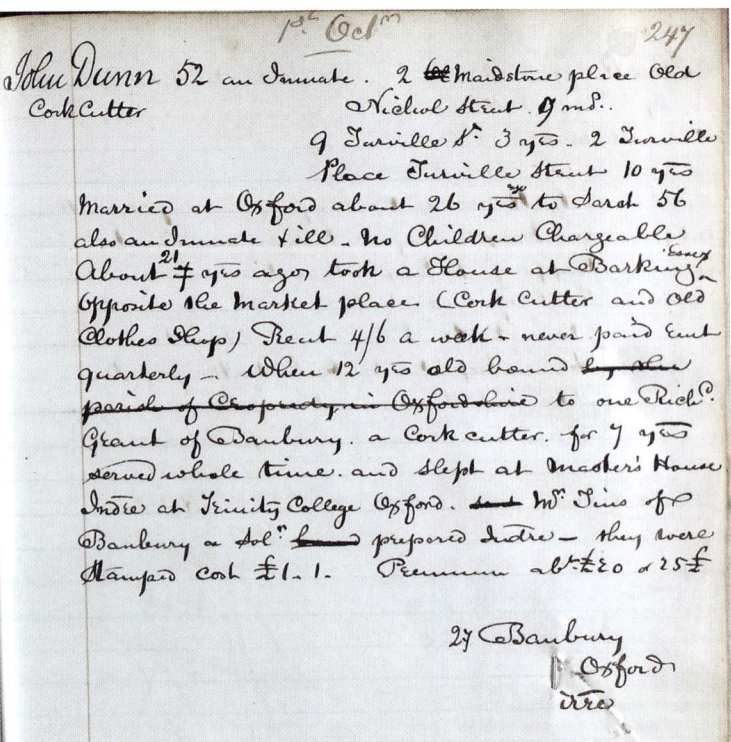

Removal Order Examination

Since 1842, the family had called Bethnal Green their home, yet an intriguing twist emerged with William's baptism taking place in Bristol, Gloucestershire. Interestingly, John consistently listed Oxford as his birthplace on census records, yet the discrepancies in his stated ages suggested a considerable range for his birth year, possibly between 1809 and 1823.

The discovery of this removal order not only gave me fresh information but also opened up exciting new avenues for research. Settlement records, including these removal orders and the settlement examinations themselves, are highly valuable sources of information and can be rich in genealogical evidence.

First, I transferred all the details from the removal order onto a mind map, ensuring that each and every piece of information was included.

The mind map on the next page details in blue all the extracted data recovered from the document itself. Each branch distinguished between the separate parts of evidence so as to make it clear and allow space to extend out further with our next steps.

What did I deduce from these facts? These are the details in the white boxes. These often appear to be repeating some of the data, but sometimes that verifies dates of events or locations thus ensuring it's clear exactly what the evidence shows.

The next step was to analyse all the evidence and deductions and plan the next steps forward. These research steps are detailed in orange on the mind map and show our aims.

Although you have your research plan, do not discard your mind map. It can now be used as a checklist for when carrying out the actual research and further facts can be noted from the websites or archives involved in the actual research. This helps you keep track of what you have done; it tells you exactly what has been searched and so allows you to remain aligned with your plan.

MIND-MAPPING MADE EASY FOR FAMILY HISTORIANS

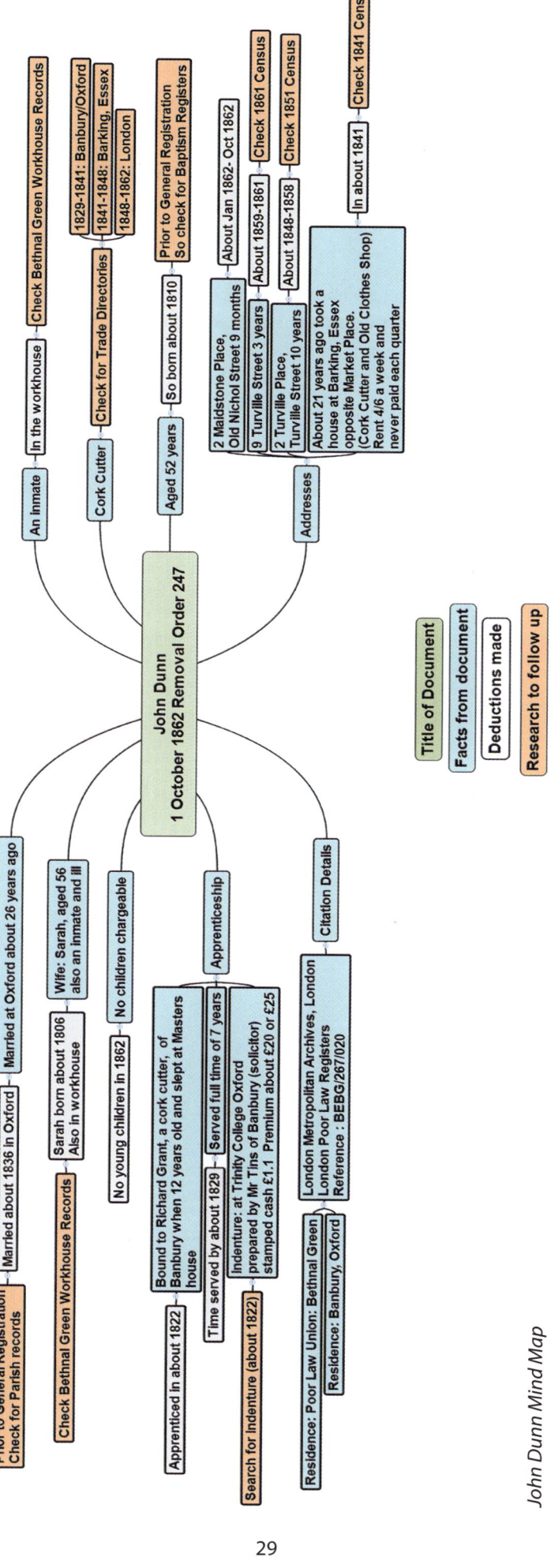

John Dunn Mind Map

Planning a research trip

For this mind map I will share with you my approach to planning a research trip to the Devon Heritage Centre in Exeter. My objective was to delve into the records of the Devon and Exeter Boys' Industrial and Reformatory Schools as part of a research project.

I wanted to ensure that I had all the information with me when I went to the archive, so included everything I considered relevant on my mind map. In terms of organisation, you will see that I put both schools on the right-hand side of the mind map, including any information about the formation, changes and closures of the individual schools.

I then used the online archive catalogues to locate all the records available for each school, their years of coverage and their access numbers and added these onto my mind map.

On the left-hand side of the mind map, I included additional essentials, such as the archive information itself, details of maps which could help me locate the schools' locations and information on books relevant to the schools.

By creating this mind map I knew that I had all the information I would need when at the archives. I had a list of all the records I wanted to access and thus a check list to enable me to mark off each record as I accessed it and extracted all the information.

The mind map's flexibility was crucial. If I uncovered new information during the archive visit, I could easily integrate it into my mind map, thus giving me an in-depth research log for not only this archival trip, but for future trips.

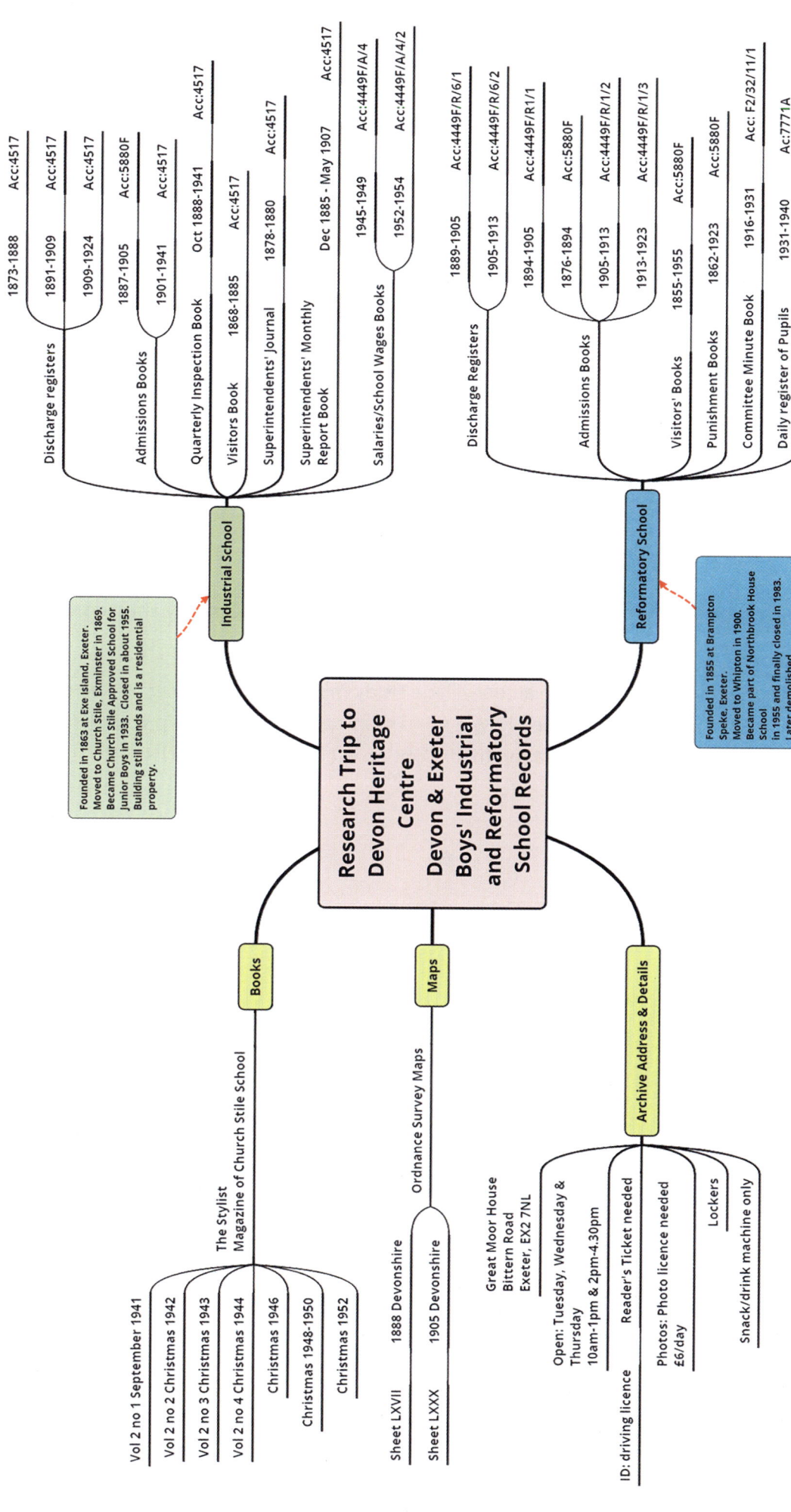

Research Trip Mind Map

Constructing a village or local study

If your ancestors lived in a small village then quite often it can be enlightening to carry out a study of the village itself, particularly if your ancestors lived in the same place over a long period of time. By studying not only the people, but also the place where your ancestors lived, you can learn so much about the social history of that place through time.

This can also be known as a one-place study, although the "place" could be a village, street, business or even a graveyard! You don't have to be an expert historian to carry out a one-place study – anyone can get involved. You may want to contact a local family history society for guidance if you don't live near the actual location yourself, and they will generally be very supportive of your work.

We are not trying to find out about a particular person with this type of research, but more about the area a person or family lived in, their way of life and the events that affected their lives. By studying where a person lived, you can see what their status was in life. You can also discover why they may have had a particular trade, or what affected people's choice of occupation in their locality.

Maybe your family lived in a village for a long period of time. Why might that be? By studying the locality and the people who lived there, you will be able to see how things have changed over the years and how this affected the inhabitants of the village.

You will be looking at a range of historical records, stories and statistics to see how they affected the lives of your ancestors thus helping you gain a deeper understanding of your own family history.

For this example, I am not going to show you an actual village study mind map, but rather a mind map for planning the research itself. This way you can see how a mind map can be used to help you plan such a project, ensuring you don't miss out any information that might be useful.

Village Study Mind Map

Carrying out a house history

As part of my genealogical study towards my degree in genealogy, I undertook a house history study of a property in Brick Lane, Spitalfields, London. House history studies are not something that all family history researchers will carry out, but they can prove to be absolutely fascinating.

There are usually two facets to the research:

- The architectural facts which include details of the construction, builder, type or style of building, materials used and changes made to the building over time.
- The historical facts which include the owners and residents of the property through time and any events associated with the building.

Some researchers will concentrate on just one type of research and some will work on a combination of the two. I chose to work mainly on the historical facts, but did include details of the architectural facts when I felt they helped my research.

By looking at the property that your ancestors lived in, and seeing how both the property and its residents have changed over time, you can get an insight into your ancestors' lives and see how they fitted into their local community and what their social standing was. This allows you to physically connect with your past family.

By using a mind map both in the planning stages of this project and then during the research process itself, I was able to contain all the information in one area, making it so much easier to see what had been found and what still needed to be done.

The final mind map shows the extent of research that was possible. The actual report itself obviously went into detail on each of the residents and the records where they appeared. The mind map did not need to contain information at that level as I was using it as a working document and did not intend to include it with my submission.

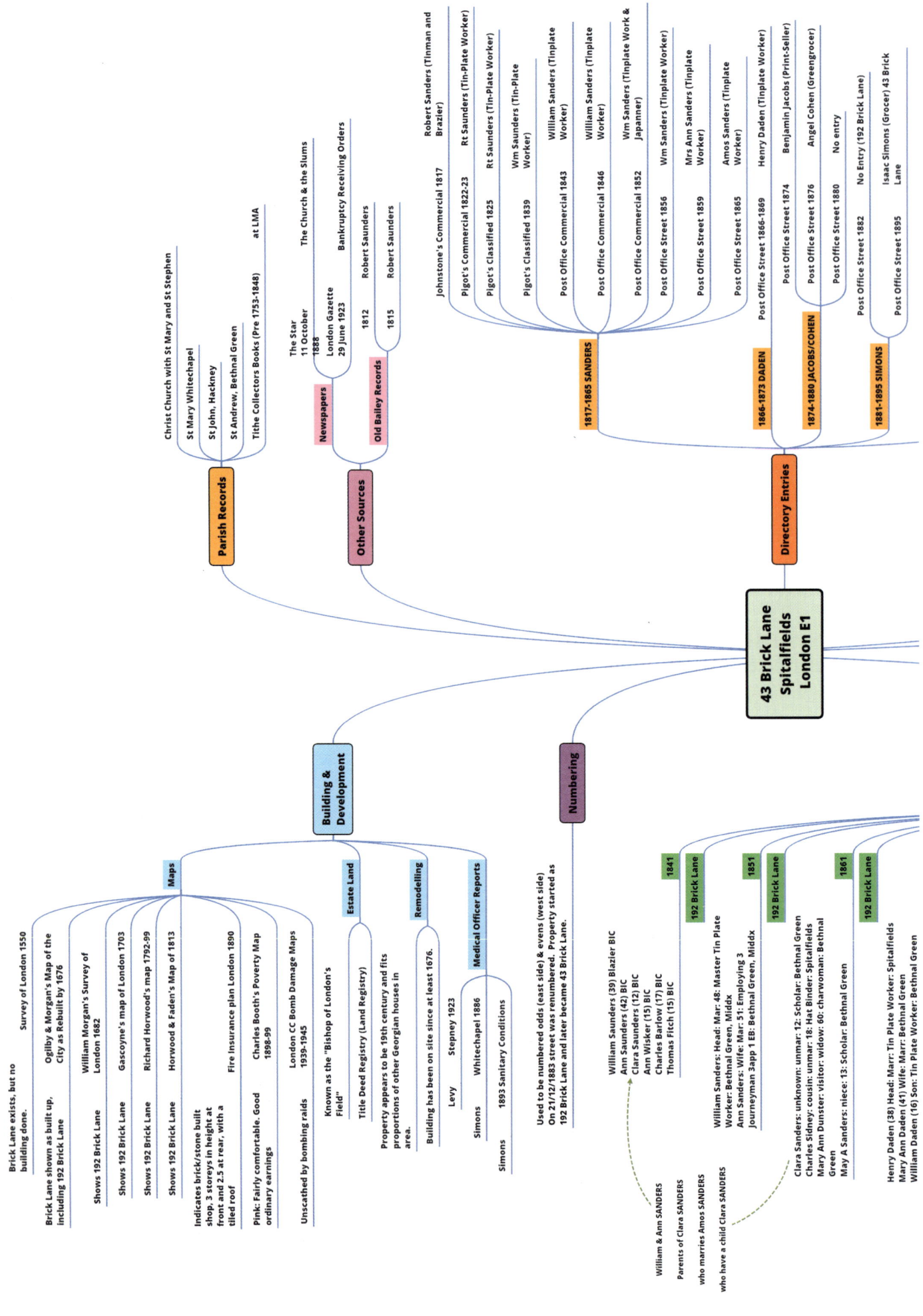

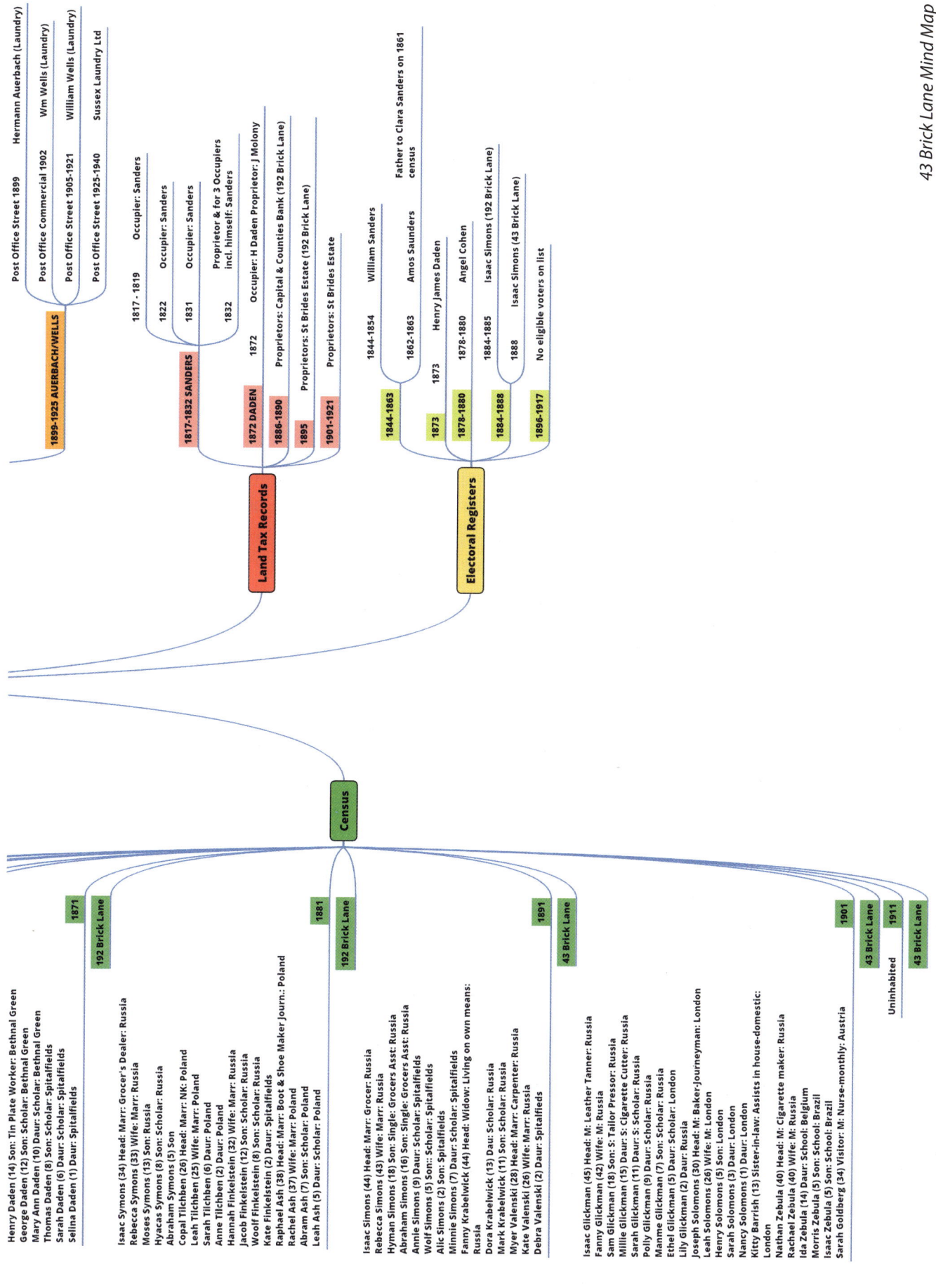

Breaking down a brick wall

Mind maps can prove invaluable when we are confronted with a familiar and often challenging obstacle in our genealogical research – the metaphorical brick wall. It could be locating that elusive person, tracking down a set of missing documents, or unravelling the intricacies of a complex family situation. The following example will illustrate how mind maps will become an indispensable tool in your armoury.

When I embarked on the journey to trace my Irish ancestry, I discovered the transformative power of mind maps in breaking down brick walls and unlocking hidden stories. My great-great-grandfather, Emanuel John Harman, a chemist born in about 1820 in Ireland, posed a significant challenge. I had no idea exactly where in Ireland he was born and only knew that he had died in 1889, in County Armagh; this is obviously prior to the 1901 and 1911 Irish censuses.

The absence of any additional records or documents further complicated matters. His marriage certificates provided scant clues regarding his parentage, merely naming Emanuel Harman as his father and offering two differing occupations for him. My great-great-grandfather remained shrouded in mystery. I needed to find a way to gather all the details I could to piece together the story of his life.

I decided to create a mind map of Emanuel John Harman's life and try and organise those fragments of information that my research revealed. In this chapter the step-by-step methodology I used will be explained; the resultant completed mind maps are too large to display here but I will show you how each branch was created and explain the process. Hopefully you will see the method behind my research and how I actually created the finished mind maps; then you will understand how mind maps were used to expand my family history and overcome the proverbial brick wall.

I began my mind map with the evidence I knew was accurate – Emanuel Harman had married twice in his lifetime, so my first branch detailed these marriage entries.

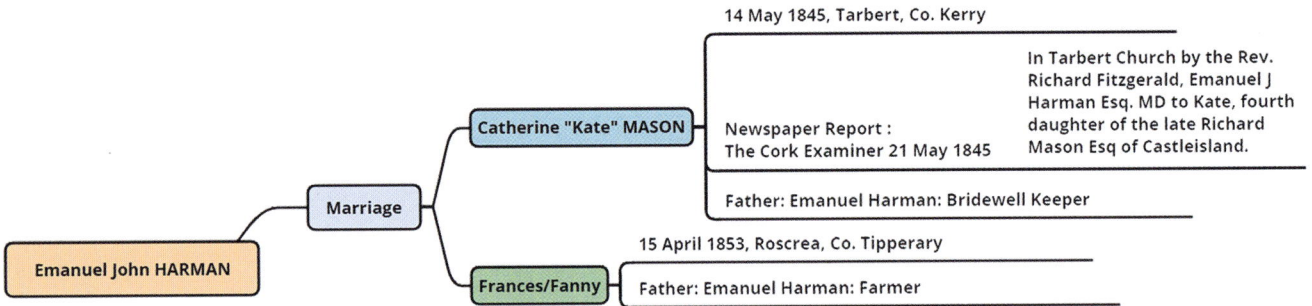

He first married Catherine Mason in 1845, stating that his father was Emanuel Harman, a bridewell-keeper. Then, in 1853 he married for a second time, giving his father as Emanuel Harman, now a farmer. He consistently gave his own occupation as a chemist on both records.

While differing occupations given for his father might seem puzzling, I considered the social context of this period. In 1845 his father worked as the keeper of the bridewell, (the local jail), and in 1853 he was a farmer; this was the exact period of the Great Famine in Ireland. There was much social change and this may have necessitated his change of occupation and transition to farming. So, I had Emanuel John Harman, son of Emanuel Harman. Not much to go on, but at least what seems like a fairly unusual first name and a not too-common occupation.

From his first marriage to Catherine Mason, two sons, Emanuel and Richard, were born. I managed to collate a good bit of research on both boys, including details of their births, and deaths. Interestingly, Emanuel emigrated to the USA and I located not only his passenger record, but also his enlistment records in the US Army.

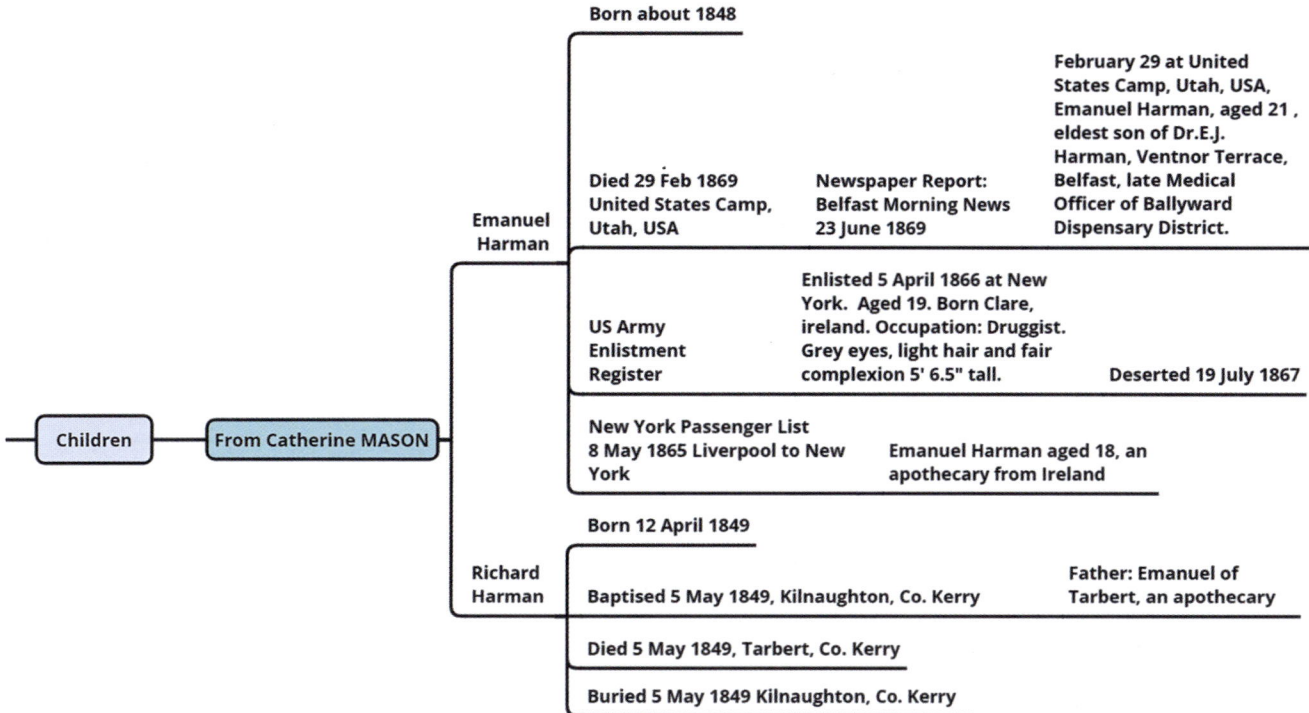

Catherine, Emanuel's wife, tragically passed away just days after giving birth to Richard. Sadly, Richard also died, both of them succumbing to cholera. The local newspapers contained announcements giving further details of the sad events.

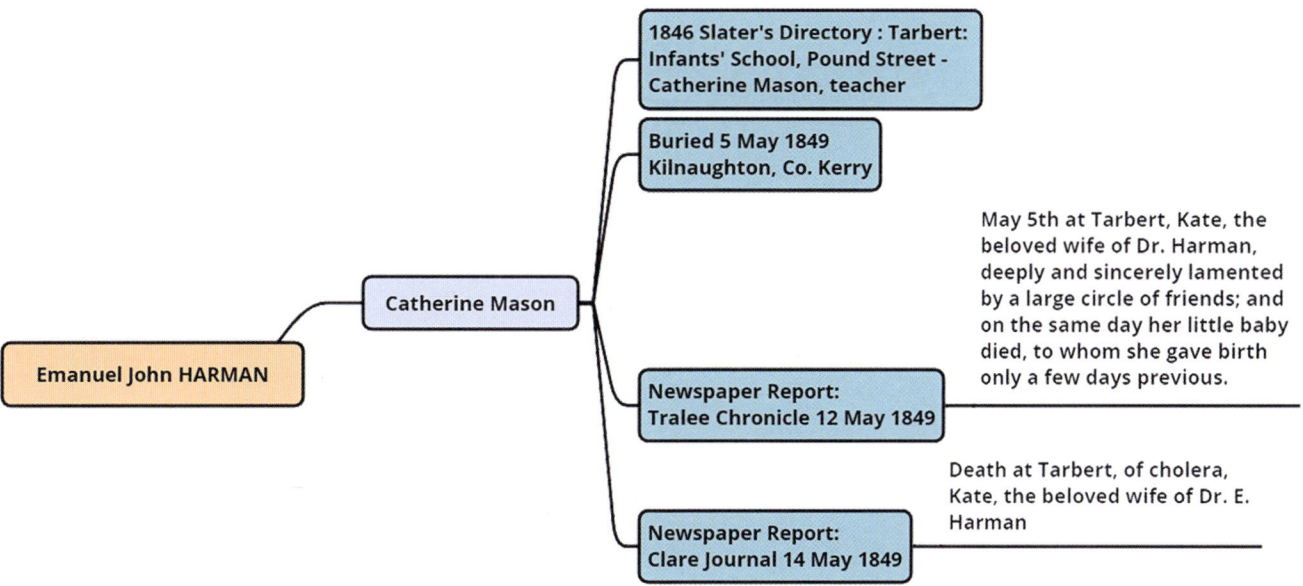

Emanuel went on to marry Frances Rudd, affectionately known as Fanny, and together they welcomed another four children into their family.

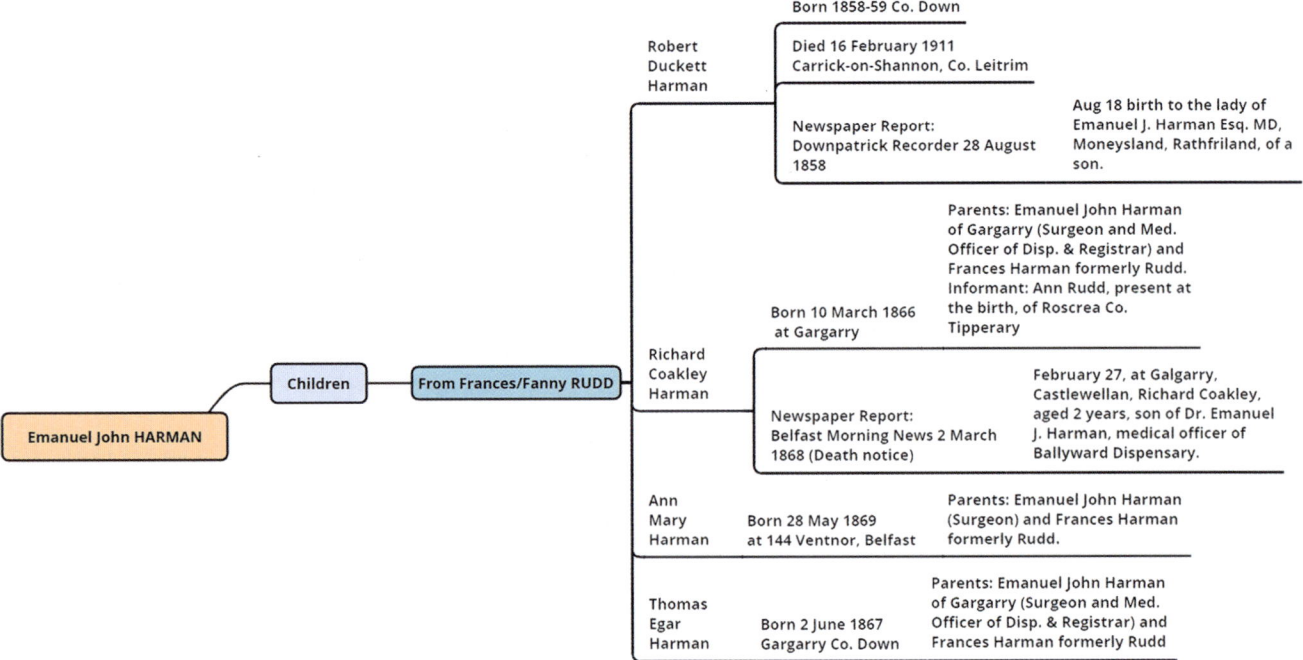

As you can see, with names like Robert Duckett, Richard Coakley, Ann Mary and Thomas Egar, I was hopeful that the more obscure names would be my line. You always hope your ancestor won't turn out to be the more common name, like Ann Mary! Luckily, I discovered that I actually descended from Robert Duckett Harman, who, like his father, also went on to train and work as a chemist.

I then went on to extend any details pertaining to Frances which might help me in later research; including details of her death record.

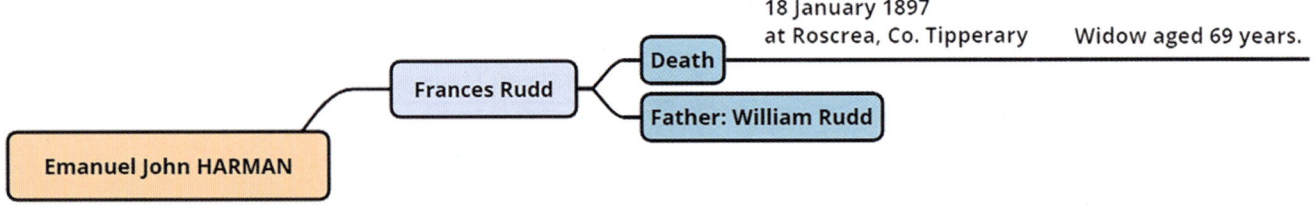

Additionally, I had unearthed directory entries providing additional insights into the life of Emanuel John Harman. These entries included not only general address details but also specific information about his occupations.

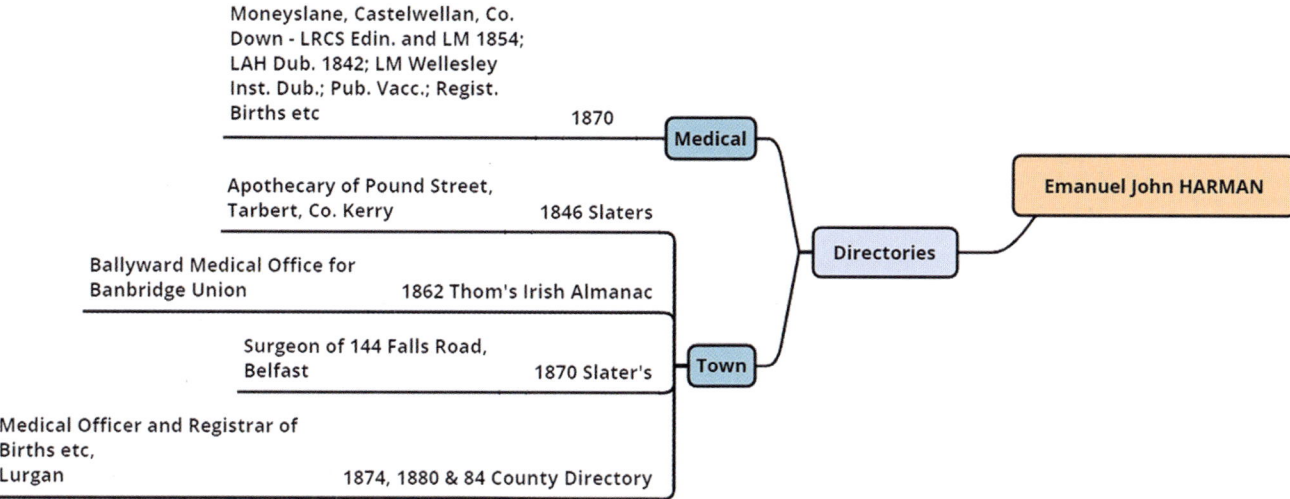

I also located death, burial and will records for Emanuel to add to the mind map. I carefully selected and edited the text to ensure that the branches weren't overwhelmed, but still had enough information to capture the main details.

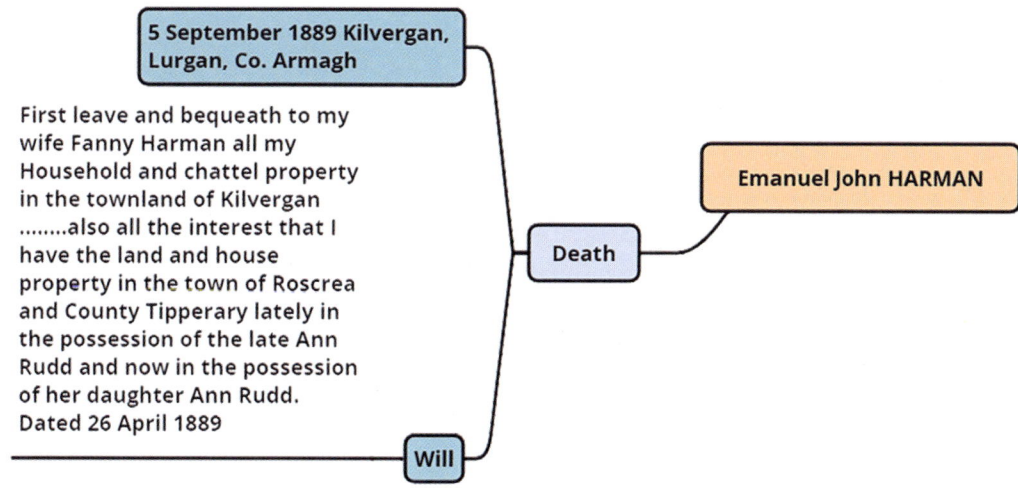

In my search for the baptism of Emanuel John Harman about 1820, only one result emerged – a baptism in 1819 in Kenmare to parents Mary and Emanuel Harman. While not definitively proved as his baptism, the closeness of the date, location and the father's name with the information I already had, made it a compelling candidate. In all likelihood, it was him.

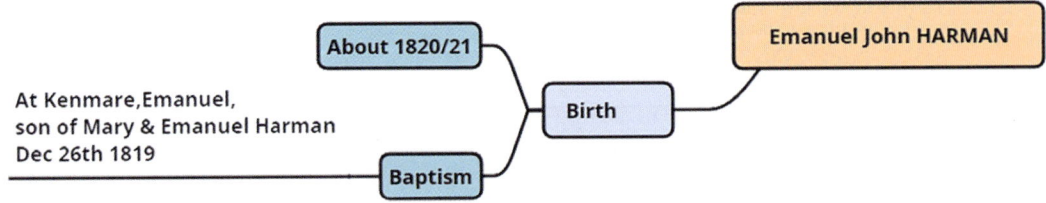

Now normally you would not add all these speculative details to a family tree in case it later proved to be the wrong baptism, however, with a mind map this is not an issue. The "probable" record of Emanuel John Harman's baptism can be assigned its own node, allowing you to keep it separate and clearly identified. If future research reveals any contradictory evidence, this specific node can be deleted at a later date without affecting the integrity of the overall mind map.

After adding the baptism details onto the mind map, I set about searching church records to try and locate any further children born to the same parents within the baptism and marriage registers.

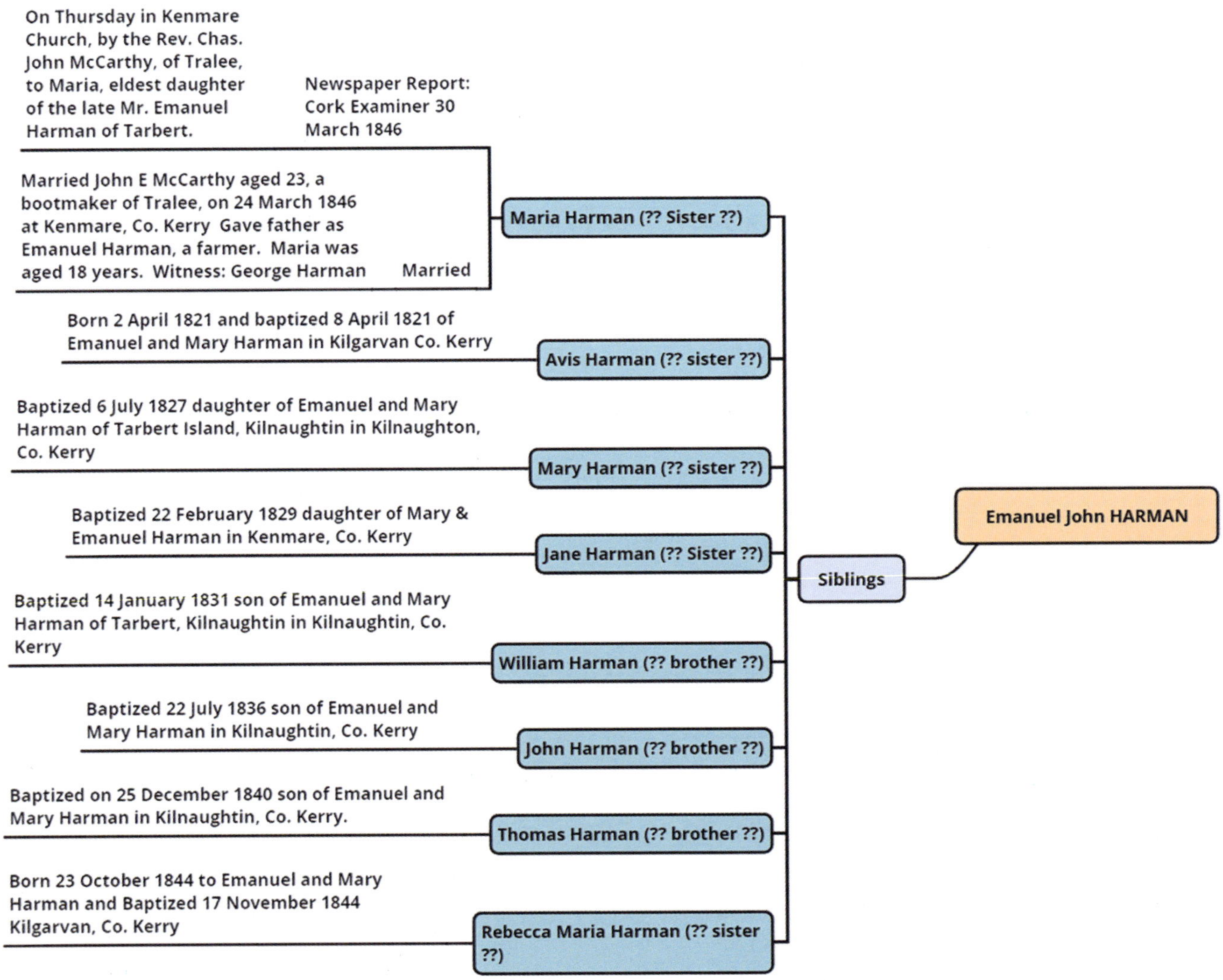

In fact, there were eight more likely siblings to Emanuel, all born to Emanuel and Mary Harman, with some entries giving more details than others. For example, the announcement of the marriage of Maria Harman to John McCarthy in 1846 was given as *John McCarthy, of Tralee, to Maria, eldest daughter of the late Mr Emanuel Harman, a farmer.* So, Emanuel Harman, her father, had died before 1846, and Maria was his eldest daughter. Maria's marriage entry also gave a witness, George Harman, someone I hadn't heard of before.

From 1821 through to 1844, each child's baptism gave me the family's location and things were starting to link together. However, I still had no conclusive proof that Emanuel, the farmer, was my Emanuel John's father.

I continued to add all the additional information I found including census substitutes, details on his wife's family and information about his work. I gathered every bit of evidence I could glean that could help me either confirm or disprove my findings.

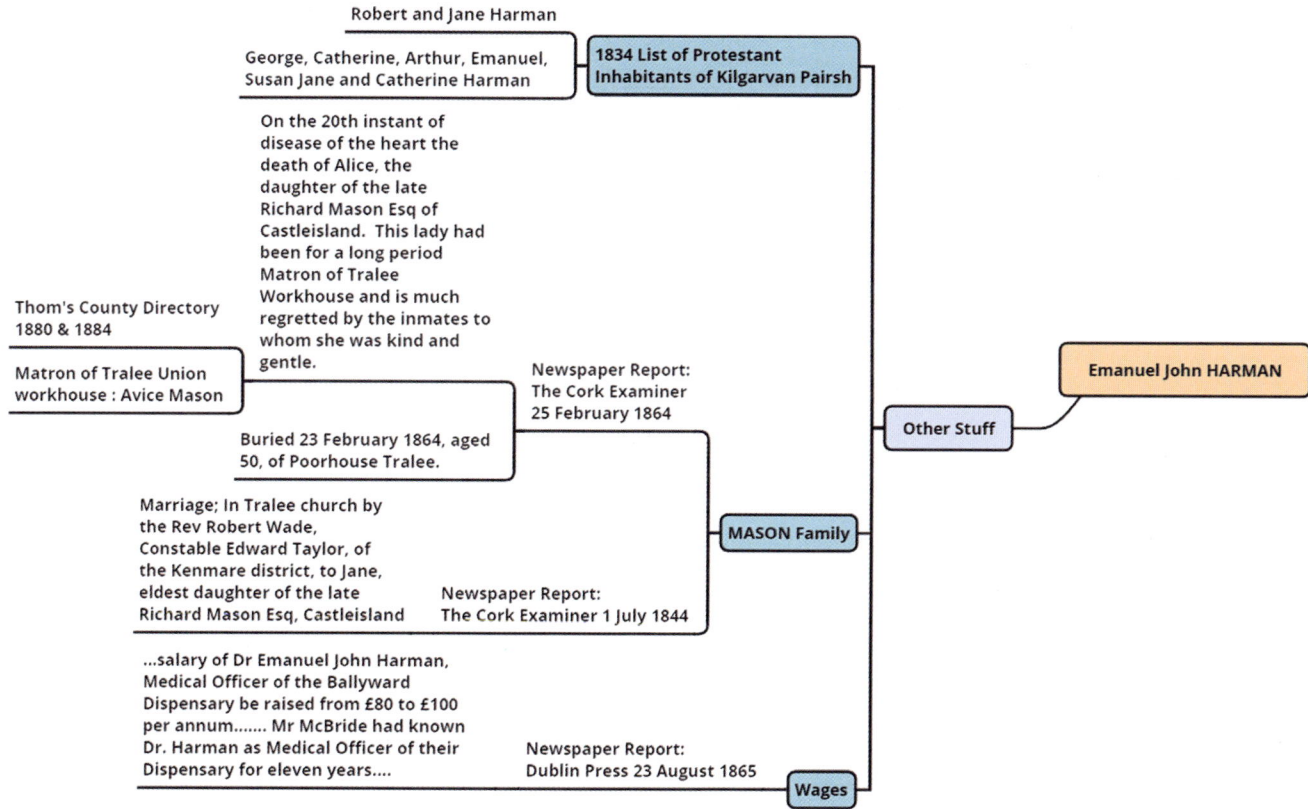

I also added in any details on other people named Emanuel Harman that had surfaced during my research. This is something that you can't normally do with standard family history software, but by doing this I ensured that I had all the evidence in one place, minimising the chance of information being overlooked or misplaced. Certain entries certainly looked as if they would be promising. The Emanuel Harman given as a bridewell-keeper between 1839 and 1844 looked possibly the same as my Emanuel Harman who had worked at the same bridewell in 1845. Others had links to the medical profession with occupations such as apothecary, druggist and even doctor being mentioned.

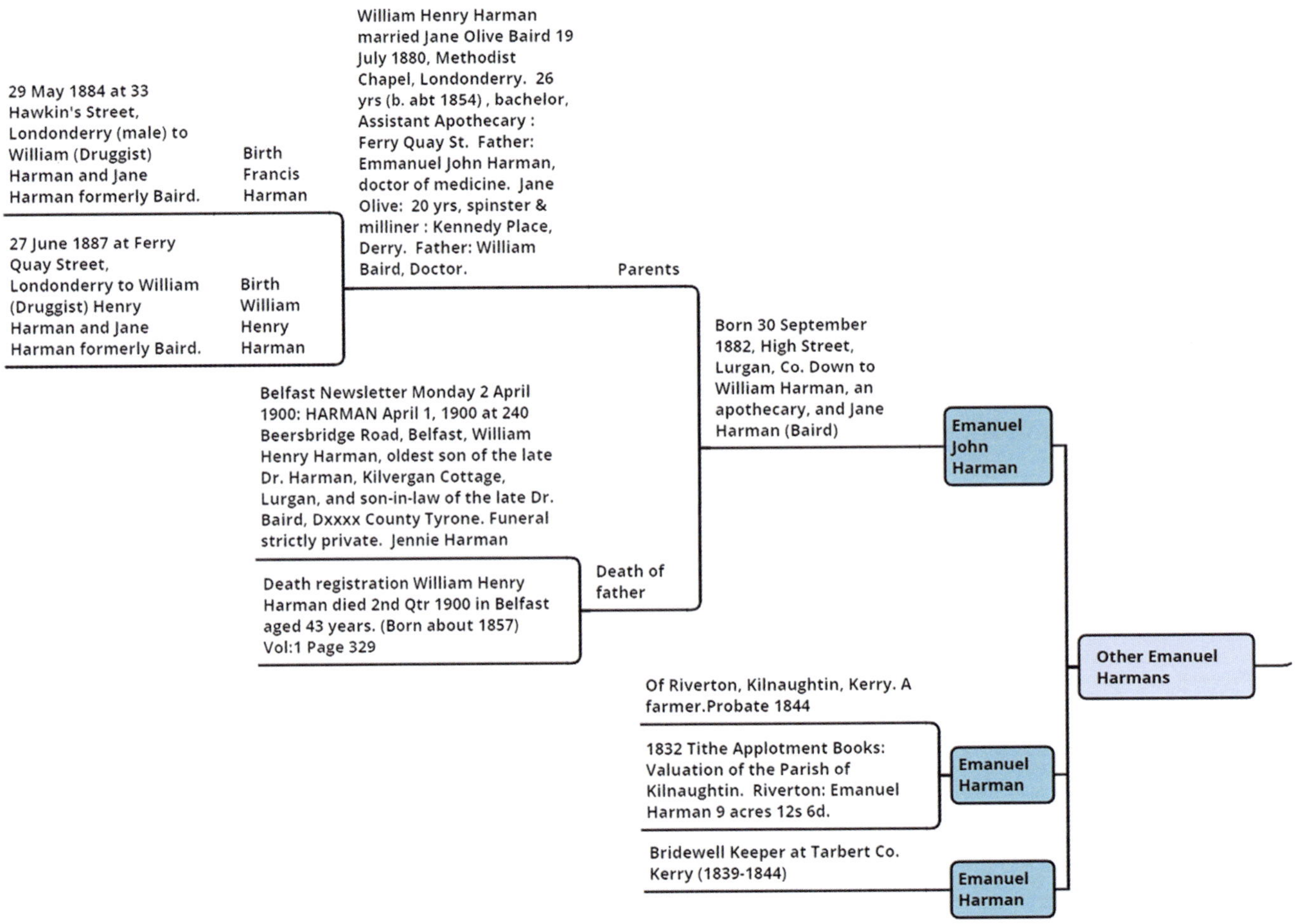

29 May 1884 at 33 Hawkin's Street, Londonderry (male) to William (Druggist) Harman and Jane Harman formerly Baird.
Birth Francis Harman
27 June 1887 at Ferry Quay Street, Londonderry to William (Druggist) Henry Harman and Jane Harman formerly Baird.
Birth William Henry Harman
William Henry Harman married Jane Olive Baird 19 July 1880, Methodist Chapel, Londonderry. 26 yrs (b. abt 1854), bachelor, Assistant Apothecary : Ferry Quay St. Father: Emmanuel John Harman, doctor of medicine. Jane Olive: 20 yrs, spinster & milliner : Kennedy Place, Derry. Father: William Baird, Doctor.
Parents
Belfast Newsletter Monday 2 April 1900: HARMAN April 1, 1900 at 240 Beersbridge Road, Belfast, William Henry Harman, oldest son of the late Dr. Harman, Kilvergan Cottage, Lurgan, and son-in-law of the late Dr. Baird, Dxxxx County Tyrone. Funeral strictly private. Jennie Harman
Death registration William Henry Harman died 2nd Qtr 1900 in Belfast aged 43 years. (Born about 1857) Vol:1 Page 329
Death of father
Born 30 September 1882, High Street, Lurgan, Co. Down to William Harman, an apothecary, and Jane Harman (Baird)
Emanuel John Harman
Other Emanuel Harmans
Of Riverton, Kilnaughtin, Kerry. A farmer.Probate 1844
1832 Tithe Applotment Books: Valuation of the Parish of Kilnaughtin. Riverton: Emanuel Harman 9 acres 12s 6d.
Emanuel Harman
Bridewell Keeper at Tarbert Co. Kerry (1839-1844)
Emanuel Harman

Emanuel's mind map had now expanded and become much larger and more detailed as I added in all available information. It was at this point that I decided to shift my focus to his son, Robert Duckett Harman, hoping that such a distinctive name would likely help in the forthcoming research.

Born in 1858, Robert Duckett Harman was recorded on the 1901 census alongside his family. Further research traced them to the 1911 census where a notable change surfaced – Robert's wife was listed as a widow.

Myra Harman, Head, 36, widow, born in Sligo
Edward Harman, son, 16, chemist's assistant, born in Roscommon
Herbert Harman, son, 15, chemist's assistant, born in Roscommon
Reginald Harman, son, 11, scholar, born in Co. Leitrim
Myra Harman, daughter, 7, scholar, born in Co. Leitrim
Rupert Harman, son, 3, scholar, born in Co. Leitrim
1911
Robert Duckett Harman
Census
Robert D. Harman, head, 43, pharmaceutical chemist, born Co. Down
Almyra Harman, wife, 29, born in Sligo
Edward Harman, son, 6, scholar, born in Co. Roscommon
Herbert Harman, son, 5, scholar, born in Co. Roscommon
Reginald Harman, son, 1, scholar, born in Co. Leitrim
1901

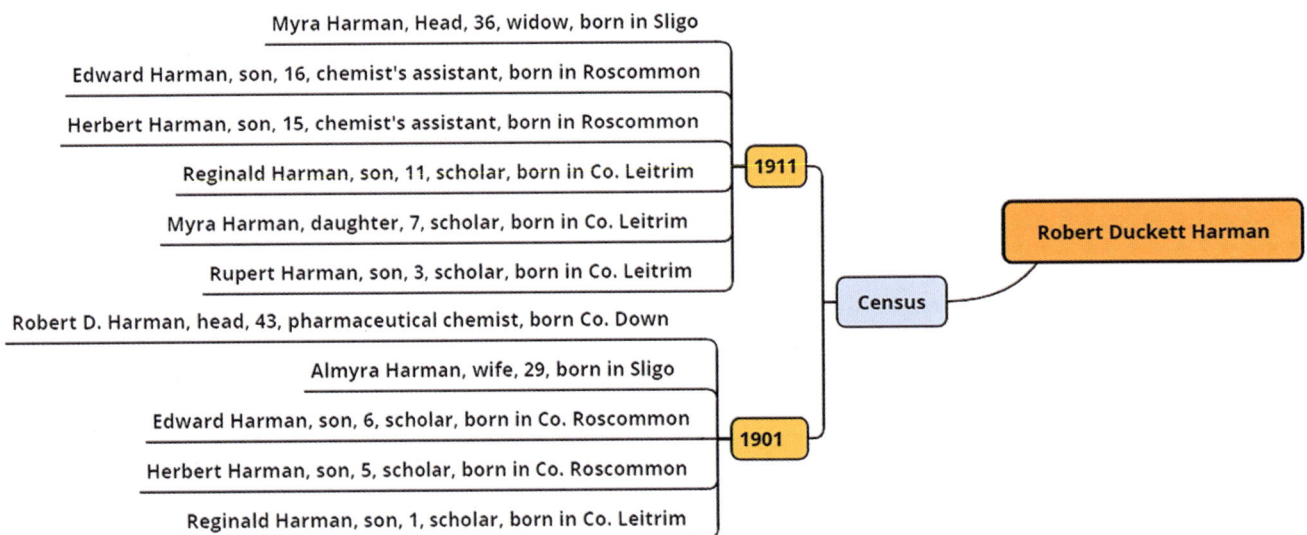

With relative ease I traced all their children from the 1901 and 1911 censuses, located details about their births as well as some information on certain marriages and deaths.

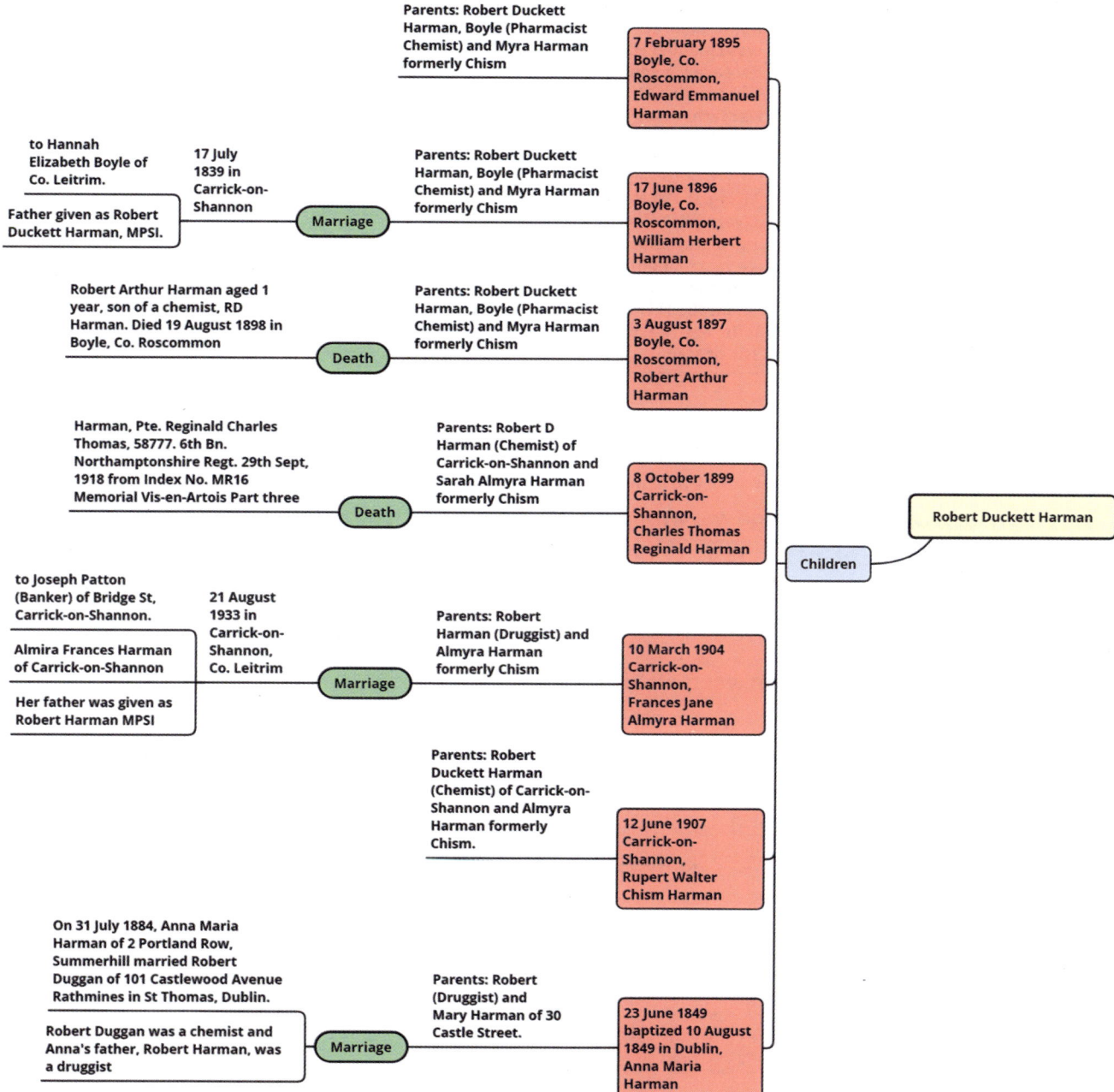

During my research, I also came across another Robert Ducket Harman, who would have been born about 1837 and who had featured on the English census of 1881 with his wife Isabella. The spelling of Duckett had only one "t", but as we all know, spellings with double letters are particularly prone to being spelled in a variety of variants. I knew my Robert Duckett Harman was born in Ireland but as far as I knew, he'd never been to England. I'd never heard of an Isabella either, so who was this Robert Ducket? Well, I simply popped him on my mind map under *odds and ends* knowing that I had filed him away should he prove useful in later research.

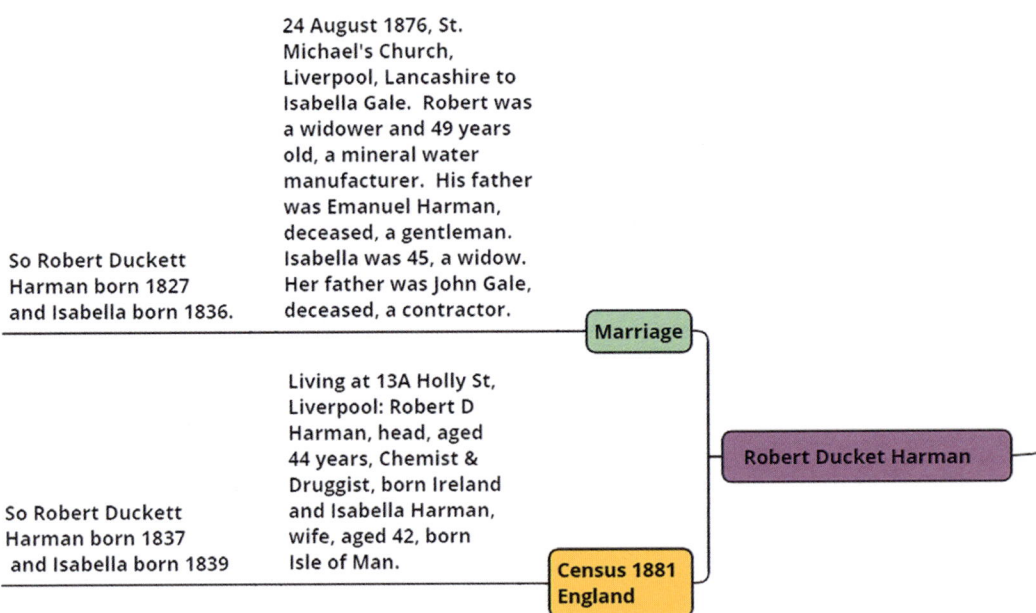

This Robert Ducket Harman was also born in Ireland and strangely was a chemist and druggist. Curious, I looked for a marriage for Robert Ducket and found it, in 1876 in Liverpool, to Isabella Gale. This obviously wasn't my Robert Duckett as the age was wrong. Despite the fact I had never heard of this particular spouse either, the commonality of the profession – being a chemist – piqued my interest. I had always presumed that the name Duckett might be a family surname perhaps inherited from his mother's maiden side of the family. So I added all this to the mind map.

Tracing my Robert Duckett Harman was quite simple due to his occupation. His life events were all reported in the *Chemist and Druggist Magazine*, a monthly journal for the pharmacy trade. I had his marriage details, his death details, even details of his wife's intention to continue running their chemist's shop after his death. This enabled me to locate his probate records. I also had confirmation that he was the second son of the late Dr Harman of Lurgan. Yes, it turned out that Emanuel Harman the chemist was actually a surgeon as well! I also located the death of a Mary Harman, who was the wife of a druggist, so added this to the deaths in the hope I could link her in later.

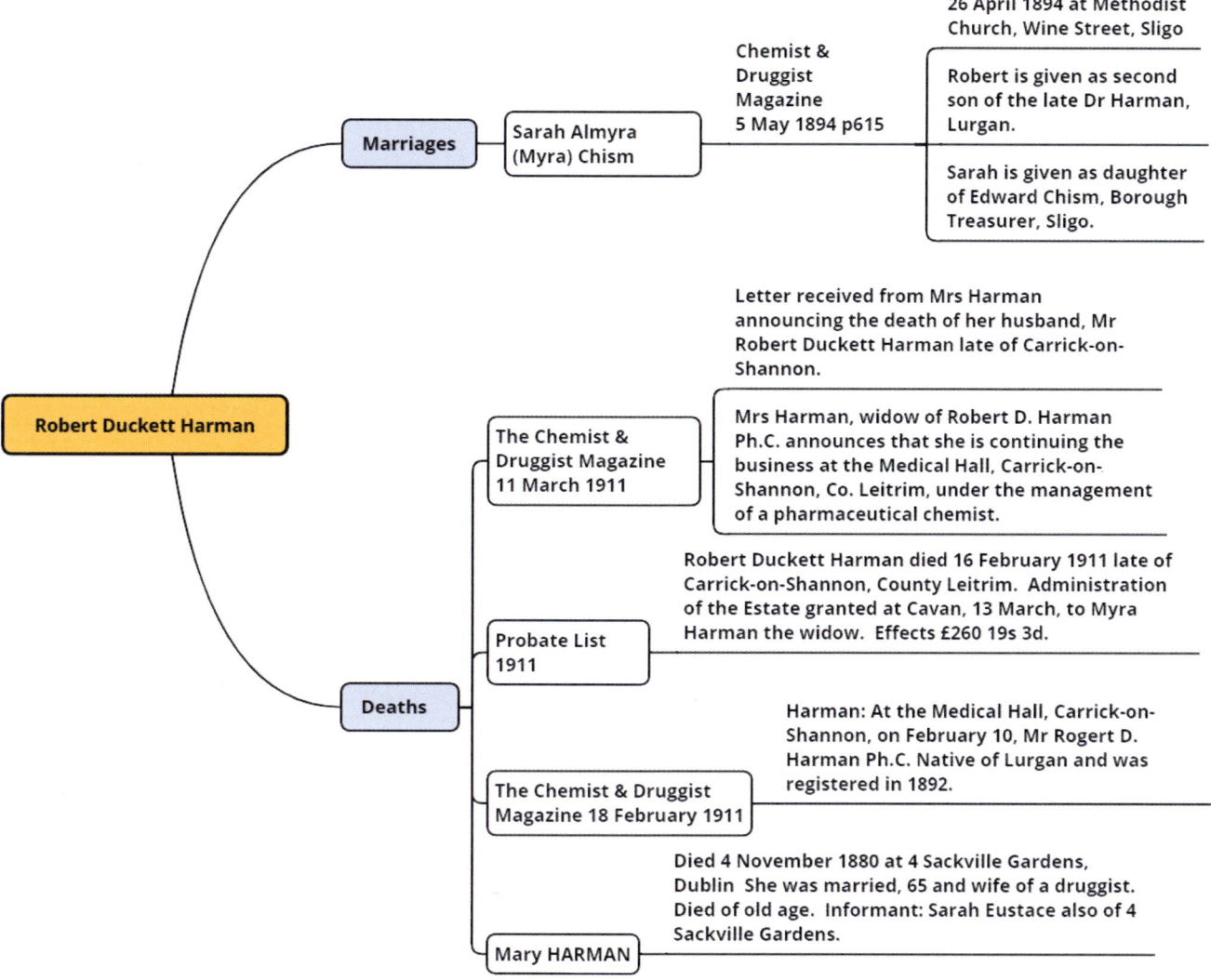

Now things weren't too complicated at this point until I found another marriage for a Robert Duckett Harman to a Mary Monks in 1847 in Dublin. This was before my Robert Duckett Harman was even born. However, his father was given as Emanuel Harman, a farmer. I promptly added him to my mind map, even though I had no idea yet where he fitted in. Noting that the street name matched that of the Mary Harman death I had found previously, I also moved the death branch of Mary Harman to this node as it seemed likely this was the same person.

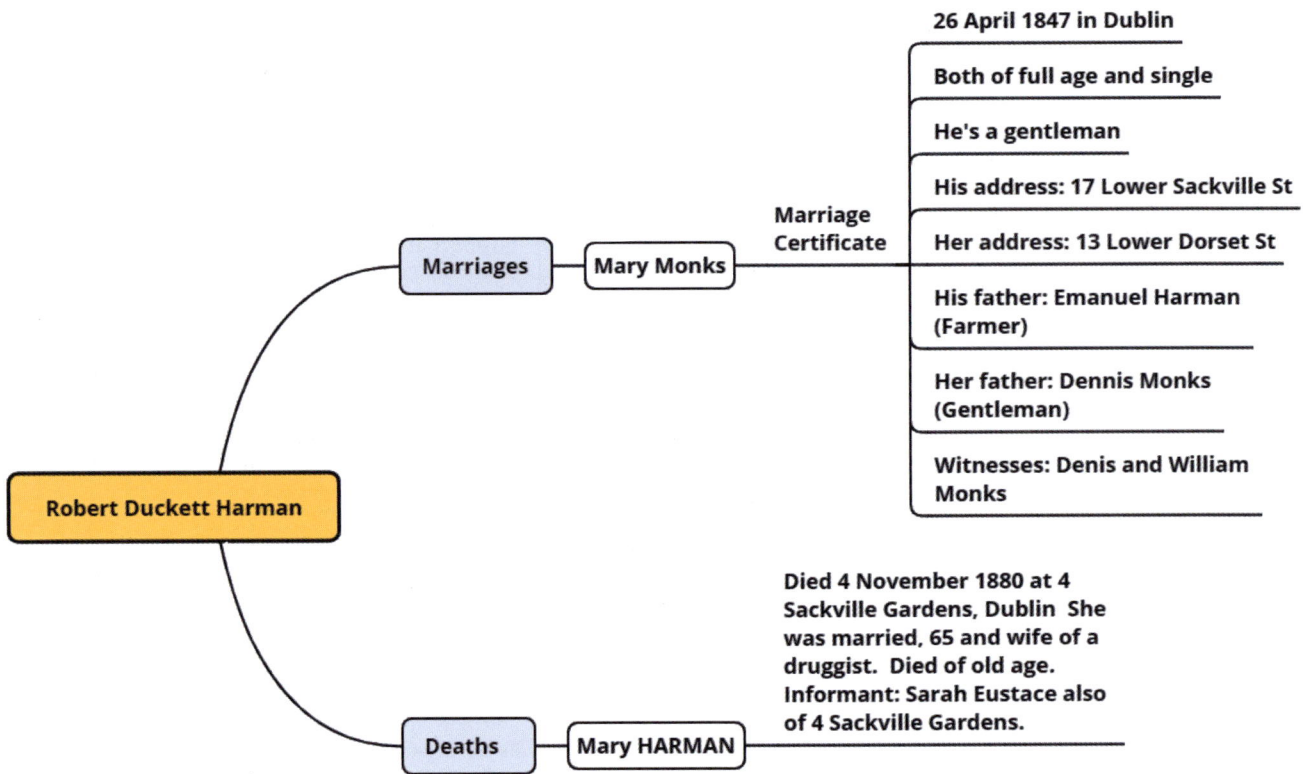

It was at this point that my mind map played a key part. There is no way all this information could have been incorporated into any type of family tree software package, or even an online tree. Scanning through the mind map, I could see that Emanuel Harman, the farmer, had had two sons, Emanuel John Harman and Robert Duckett Harman, both of whom were chemists. Emanuel John Harman, the chemist, also had two sons, Robert Duckett Harman, who was also a chemist, as well as Emanuel Harman. Talk about keeping the names in the family! This was becoming quite a tangled web, but the mind map was at least keeping me on track and organised.

Thinking back to Emanuel's mind map, when I listed his siblings, you will remember there was no Robert Duckett Harman shown.

As we'd said before, my Robert Duckett Harman had never lived in Dublin that I knew of and I had his children's births and marriage details, none of which took place in Dublin. Or had they?

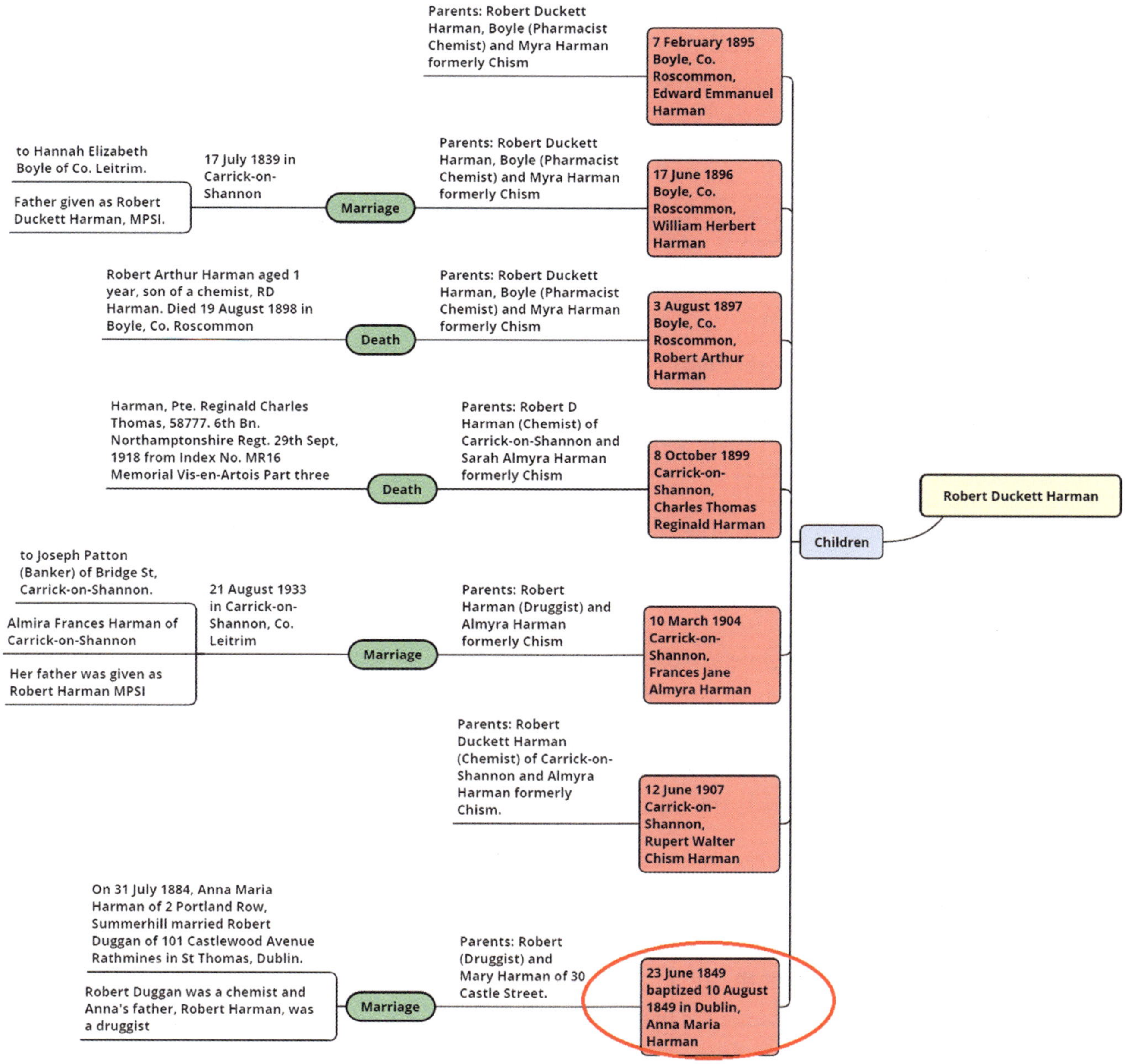

Revisiting that part of my mind map I saw that Anna Maria was born in Dublin to Robert and Mary. Now logically her mother should have been called Myra, the same as all the other children's entries, but I'd assumed when I noted it down there'd been an error and that they'd misspelt her name. But no, the address, 30 Castle Street on Anna's baptism was the same as the address in Thom's directory 1852 for Robert Duckett Harman, Chemist, Druggist and General Merchant. That was six years before the birth of my Robert Duckett Harman!

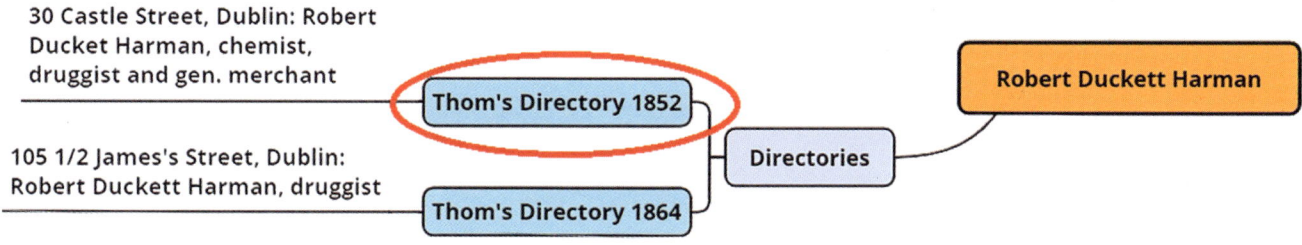

I also found a newspaper report of Robert Duckett Harman's insolvency petition in 1850, when living at Castle Street.

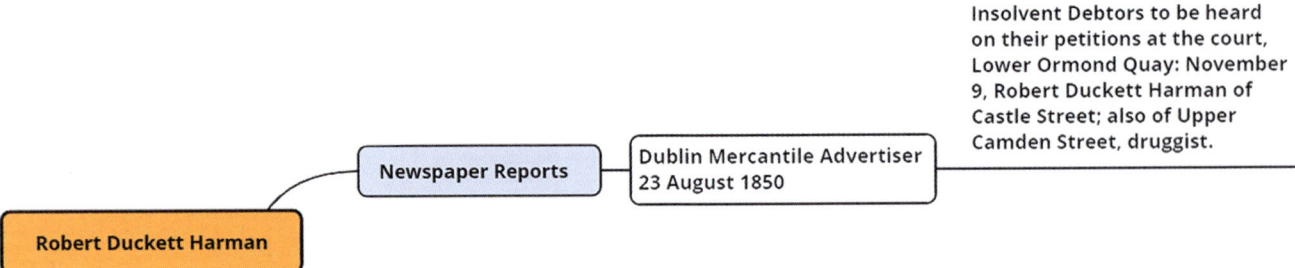

So, there were definitely two different Robert Duckett Harman's with fathers called Emanuel. There is no way I could have entered this into my family tree software without having to put lots of question marks for everything. On the mind map I could put it all on and then move the information about when things became clearer.

I honestly thought I'd cleared up this little brick wall, until I decided to check there were no other Robert Duckett Harmans in other countries that I may have overlooked. After all we did have the Emanuel Harman that was in the US Army, so perhaps other family members had emigrated as well?

So, imagine my surprise when I came across a Duckett Harman in America. I initially found his death certificate in Pennsylvania in 1921. American death certificates are wonderful because they give you so much information, but this one really threw a spanner in the works! He was born on 19 August 1838 in Ireland. He worked as an optician and his parents were Emanuel J. Harman and Hannah Duckett, both of whom were born in Ireland. So, who on earth was this Duckett Harman?

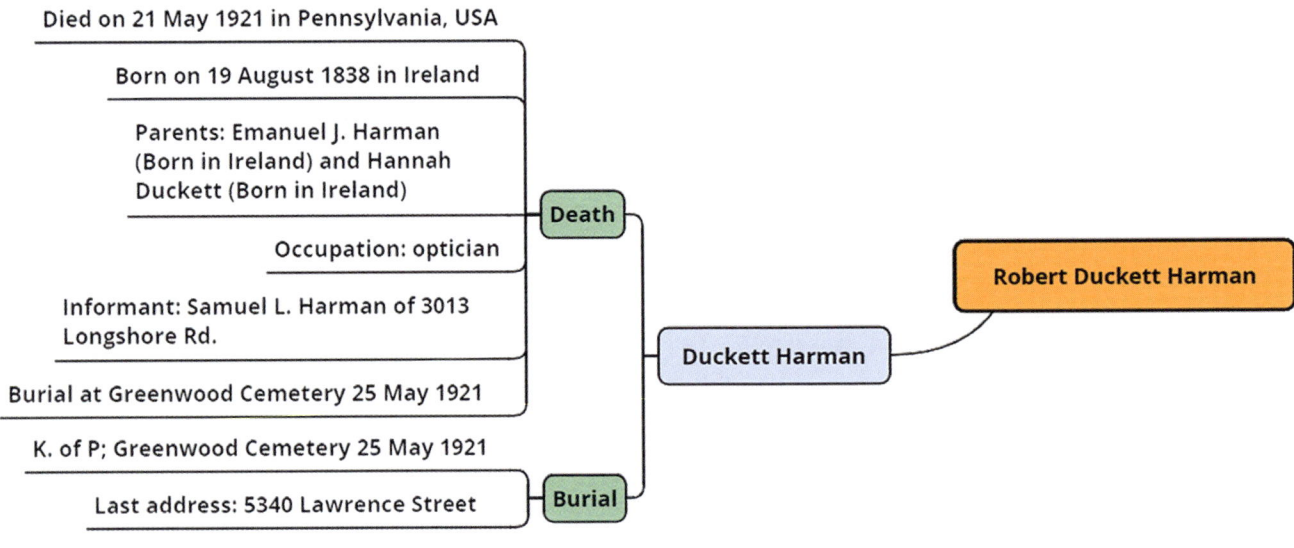

Now remember my Robert Duckett Harman was born in 1858 and my "alternate" Robert Duckett Harman was born in 1837.

I carried out some in-depth research and found the census records from 1870 right up to 1920 for this Duckett Harman and added them to the mind map.

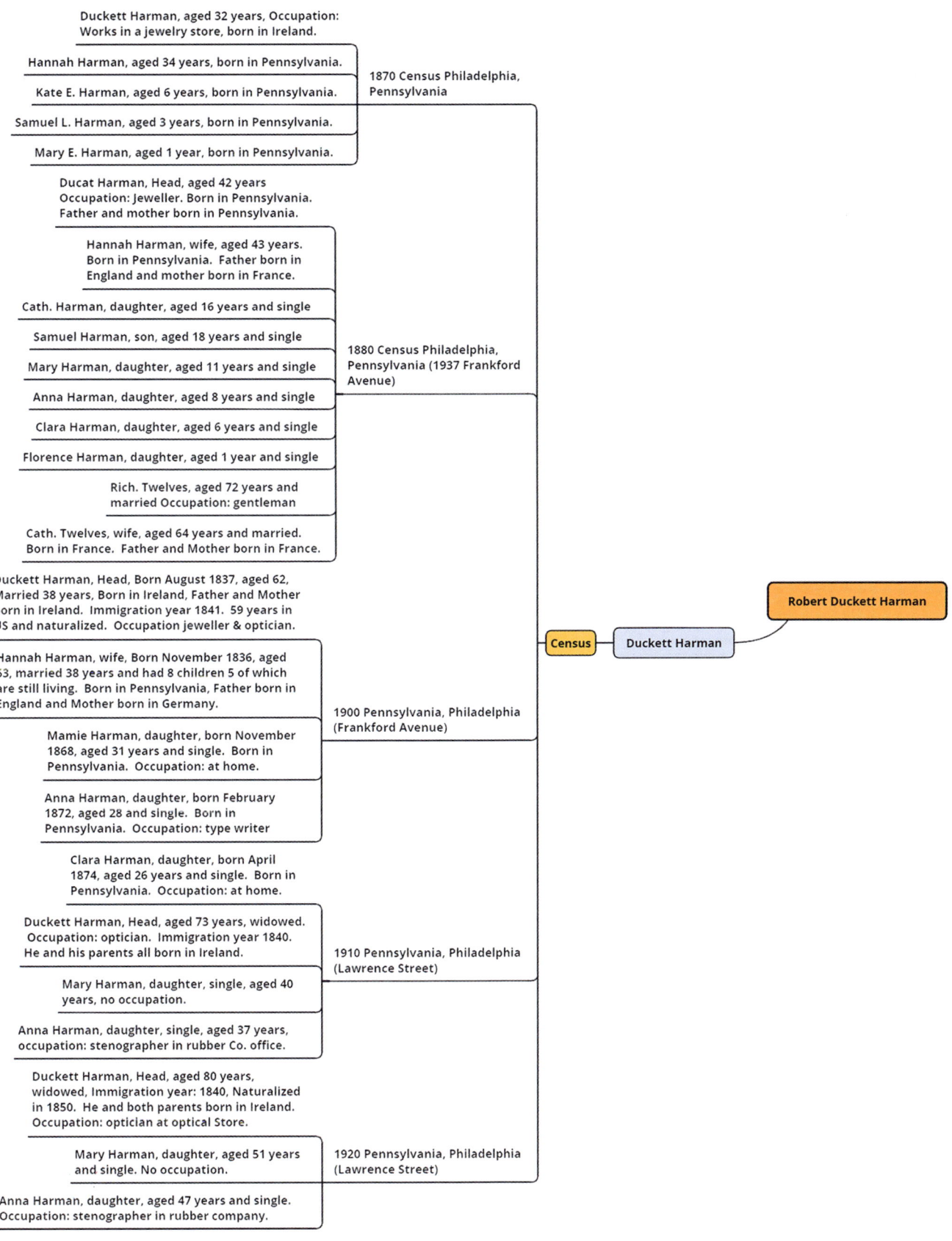

I located the marriage and death details for both Duckett Harman and his wife Hannah.

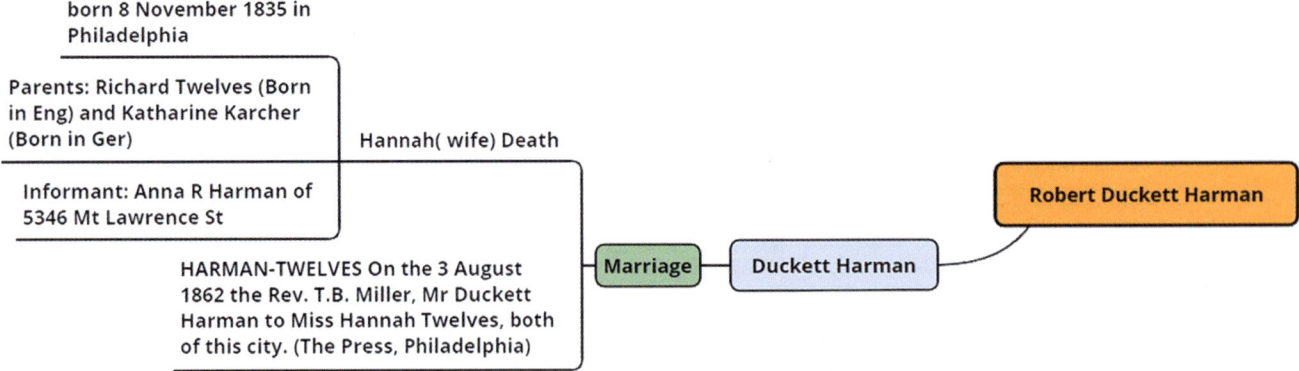

Church records revealed their membership of the Episcopal Church in Philadelphia.

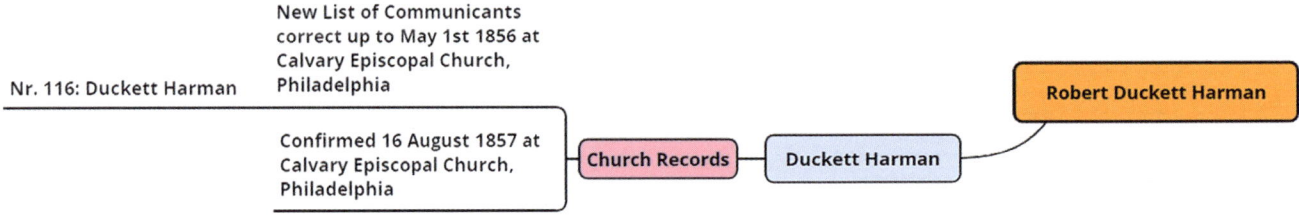

Military records detailed Duckett's enlistment record.

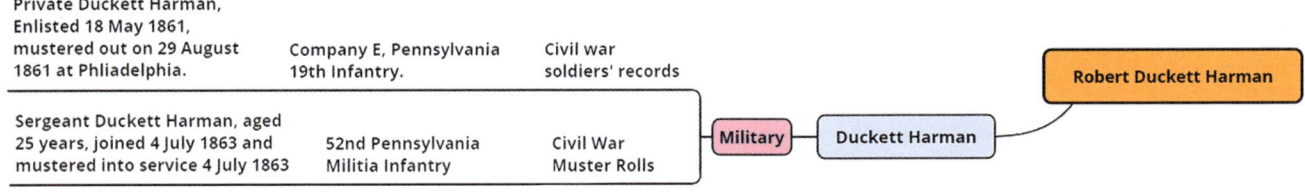

Searches of directory entries yielded more occupational records and addresses.

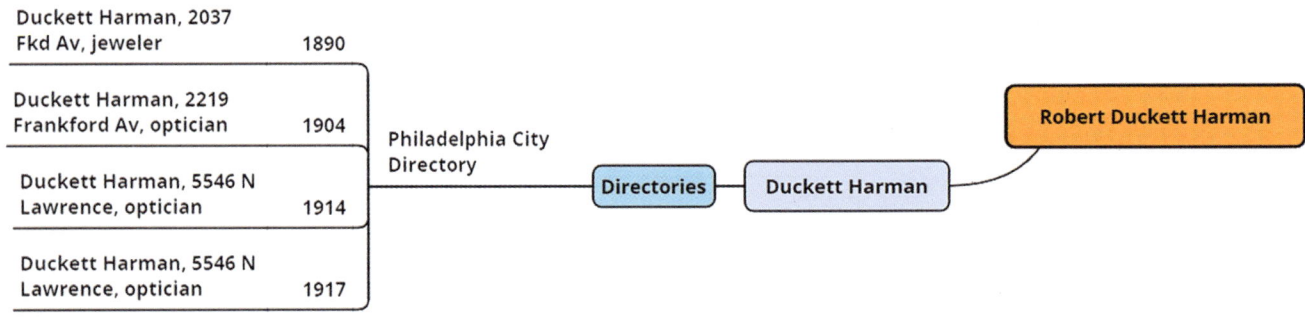

I also researched their children, locating both a baptism record for one and a death record for another.

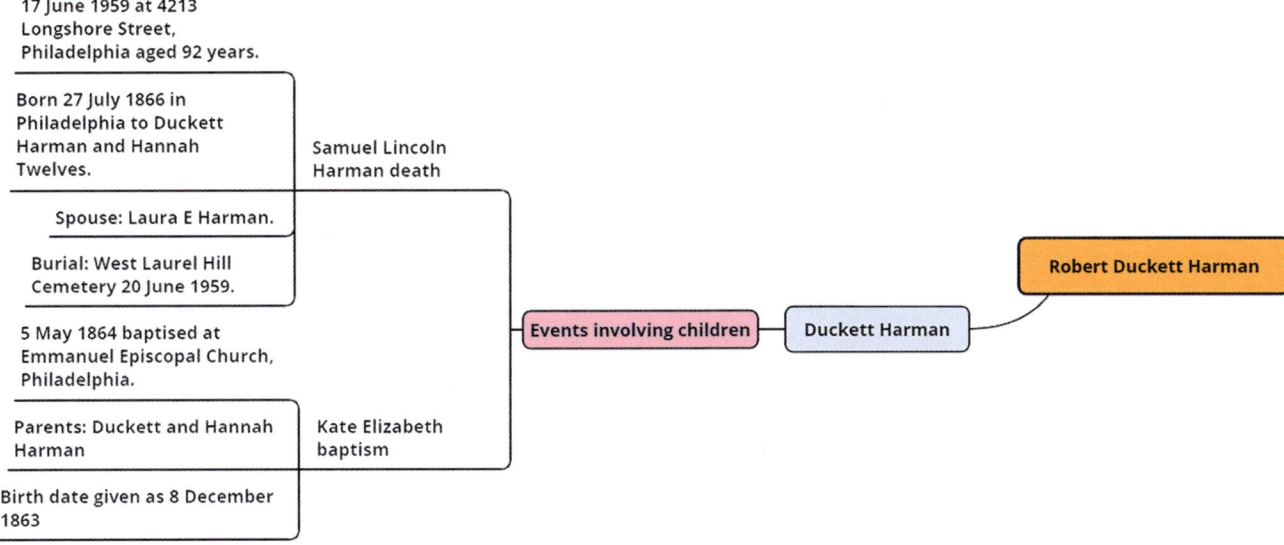

So, it appeared that this Duckett Harman was not one of my other Robert Duckett Harmans, but an entirely different one!

While doing all this research, I found various odds and ends; little notes which I wanted to keep but really didn't know where they fitted. As I said before, those things you pop on a sticky note or scribble on a page at the back of your file, leaving them to get lost or forgotten.

Firstly, I came across a Richard Topham Harman born about 1822. His father was not an Emanuel or a Robert Duckett, so why was he of interest? The witness at his marriage was one Robert Duckett Harman and that marriage was in Dublin. So, it appears our Dublin-based Robert Duckett Harman has a connection to this Richard Topham Harman. I therefore gathered what information I could about Richard Topham Harman and added it to my mind map.

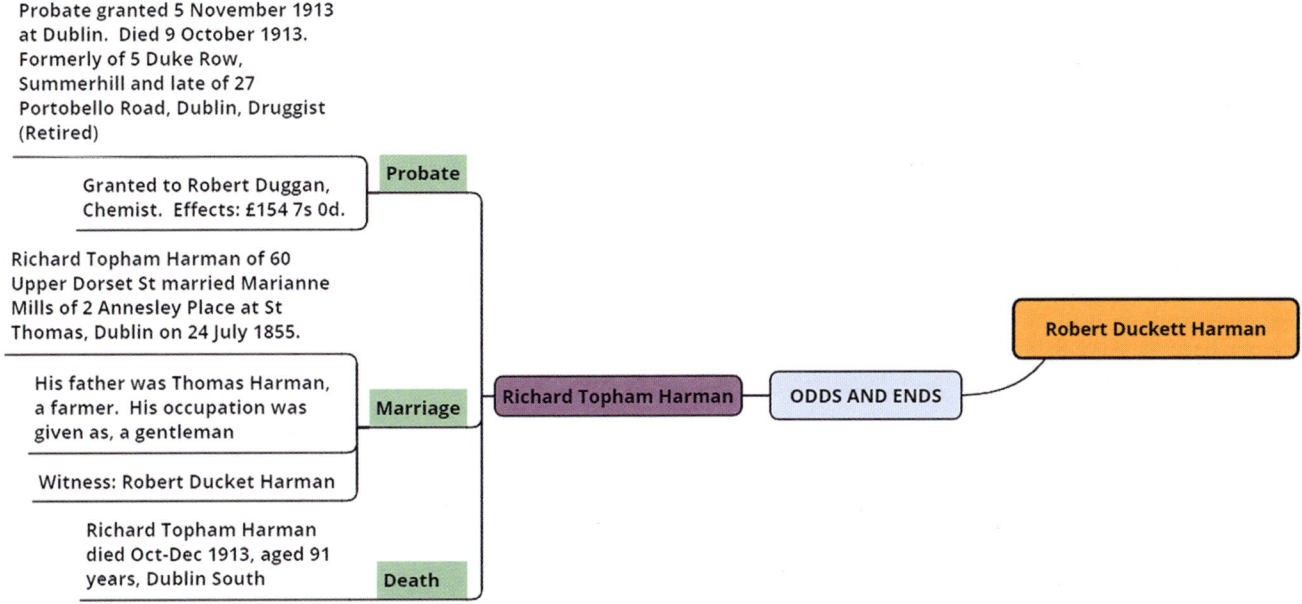

Secondly, I found a Robert Thomas Harman – again, no mention of an Emanuel or Robert Duckett but he was from Co. Down and his father was a William Harman, a chemist.

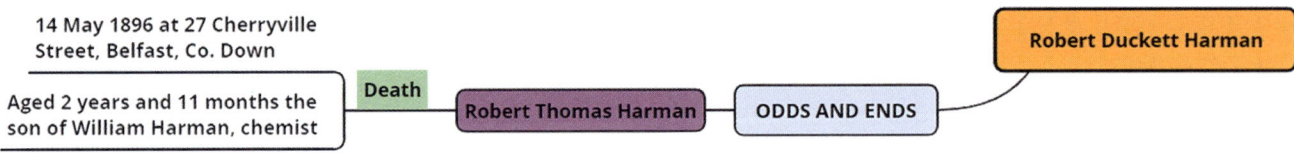

That piqued my interest as back on my Emanuel John Harman mind map, I had found an "odd" Emanuel John Harman born in 1882 to William Henry Harman, an apothecary, and Jane Olive Baird.

William Henry Harman, married in 1880 and gave his father's name as Emanuel John Harman, a doctor of medicine. Things are starting to click!

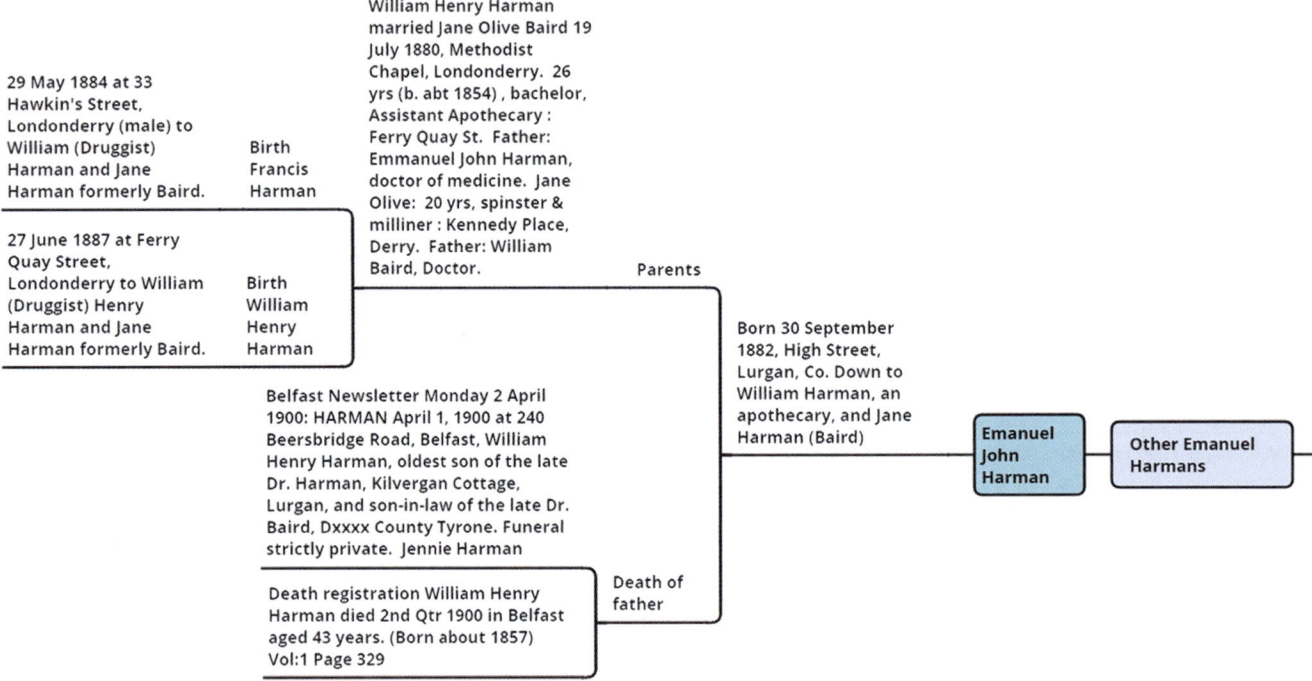

Lastly, I found a 1901 census entry for an Isabella Harmon, you remember the Liverpool Harmans? She was given as a widow, so I knew that this Robert Duckett Harman had died prior to 1901.

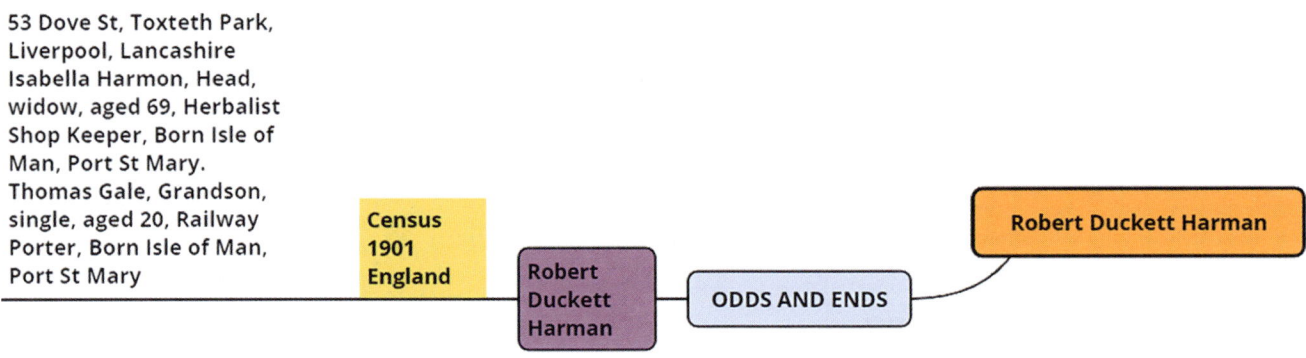

None of these facts could be stored anywhere on a traditional family tree, but all were of interest and each would have a part in unravelling the mystery of the Emanuel Harmans.

So, combining all the information I had on my Emanuel and Robert Duckett Harmans, could I connect them together or agree they were different people, and how did all those Emanuel and Robert Duckett Harmans look on one page of paper?

With all the information on what was now an extensive mind map, I was able to start linking people together. Analysis of the evidence was simplified by the fact that all the information was in front of me in one place. I could clearly locate individuals, make comparisons between data and extract information simply and with ease.

To simplify my findings and enable me to explain the evidence, I have created a picture matrix on the next page. However, it is evident when you go through the previous construction images of the mind map that I'm literally only displaying it this way to show you how the mind map separates things out for you. I've included all the pertinent information which helps us identify the separate people.

As you can see, it transpires that there were indeed four separate Emanuel or Emanuel John Harmans who each had a son called Robert Duckett or just Duckett Harman, all with very similar occupations.

Do you remember the William Harman, who had a son called Emanuel John Harman in 1882, also had a father, Emanuel John Harman, a doctor of medicine? I carried out a search on my now rather large mind map (yes, you can keyword search mind maps!) for Kilvergan; William's father was said to be from Kilvergan in his newspaper obituary, and I found that this was where two of my Emanuel John Harman's siblings were born and where he stated he held land in his will. I had a possible sibling called William already for Emanuel but he was baptised in 1831 and my William died in 1900 aged forty-three years, so he was born about 1857.

So, it appears that William Henry Harman is my Robert Duckett Harman's elder brother. The fact that I have never found a birth record for him does not perturb me. My own mother had four brothers and out of the five siblings only two had their births registered. So, it was not uncommon even in the 1930s not to register a birth.

Thus, from a rather chaotic pile of research material, I have not only separated out the four Emanuel/Robert Duckett Harman families but also managed to understand my own ancestors in much more detail. And I now have all the information I need in an organised format that I can access in a click.

Emanuel John Harman

Wife: Hannah Duckett

Both Emanuel & Hannah born in Ireland

Emanuel Harman

Emanuel Harman

Emanuel dead by 1876

Dr. Emanuel John Harman

Emanuel born about 1819 & died 1889 Co. Armagh

Married (1845) Catherine Mason, Tarbert, Ireland.
Married (1853) Francis Rudd Tipperary, Ireland.

Duckett Harman

Born : 1838 Ireland

Married : 1862 USA to Hannah Twelves

Hannah born 1835 in Philadelphia

Duckett died 1921 in Philadelphia

Emigrated to USA 1840/41

Robert Duckett Harman

Full age in 1847

Married : 1847 Dublin to Mary Monks

Mary born 1815

Mary died 1880 in Dublin

Anna Maria born 1849 Dublin, married Robert Duggan, druggist 1884 in Dublin

Robert Duckett Harman

Born : 1827-37 Ireland

Married : 1876 Liverpool, England to Isabella Gale
Widower and widow

Isabella born 1839 Isle of Man

Isabella in Liverpool on 1901 census as widow with Thomas Gale, grandson aged 20 born Isle of Man

Robert Duckett Harman

Born : 1858/59 Co. Down, Ireland

Married : 1894 Ireland to Sarah Almyra Chism (Methodist Chapel)

Sarah Almyra born 1871 Ireland

Sarah died 1948

Robert Duckett died 1911 in Co. Leitrim, Ireland

CHAPTER 9

MIND-MAPPING SOFTWARE

As you've seen you can choose to draw your mind map yourself or you can use a software package; you may even decide to use a combination of the two.

Ultimately, some of you may love mind maps but still decide to work with pen and paper. That's your choice and sometimes I do just that if I know it's going to be a relatively simple mind map. However, if you're going to work with pen and paper, there are still some points to bear in mind:

- Always work on plain paper. Lined or squared paper will limit your flow and also spoil the overall effect.
- Make sure the paper is big enough. You will need the space as your ideas and facts expand. It's better to start with a page of A3-sized paper and find you have too much space, than start with A4 and run out.
- Use the paper in a landscape position; that is best as it allows your work to flow across the page more easily.

The main limitation to using pen and paper is the inability to move things around on your mind map without resorting to rubbing out and rewriting. That is where the software packages really come into their own.

So, let's have a look at the types of programs available to create your mind maps. There are several packages available, but I will limit my analysis to those you can use on your desktop. I will not be looking at mobile applications, nor will I include software purely available for iOS or more business-orientated packages.

There are additional things you can add to your mind maps but these vary with the different software packages. Some of the things you can add are starting templates; pictures and clip art; hyperlinks; various available structures and charts; slide-based presentations; exporting functions to other software including MS Office; PDFs and varying image formats.

Some of you will prefer to download a program and keep all your files on your computer; others may prefer to work online and store all the data online for easier access. It all depends on how you work.

I have tried my best to make sure that I've replicated the same mind map in each package so that you can see how they compare. In addition, I have not changed any of the original settings, including box styles, fonts and colours. Thus, if you were to start using each package, the style you see is the style you would get without selecting any options or making any style changes. I have also used the free version, where applicable, so you can see the various watermarks or package declarations which will exist until you pay for the package.

The best thing to do is to try out some of the packages and see which one suits your way of working. The general design functions are very similar between each program. You start with a central node, label it and then by pressing "tab" you'll get a new sub-node. To get another sub-node at the same level you generally press "return" again. To extend any sub-node out to the next level on the branch, you will generally press "tab" again. This works for ninety per cent of programs I have tried.

The list I have given is not exhaustive. There are other packages out there and new ones are always being brought to the market, so if none of these suit your style, have a look around online!

Mindmeister Map

	Price	Availability	Access	Website
MindMeister	Free (limited space) Paid (Unlimited use)	Web application and mobile versions for Android and IOS	Online and web-based	www.mindmeister.com/

Mindmeister Grid

MIND-MAPPING MADE EASY FOR FAMILY HISTORIANS

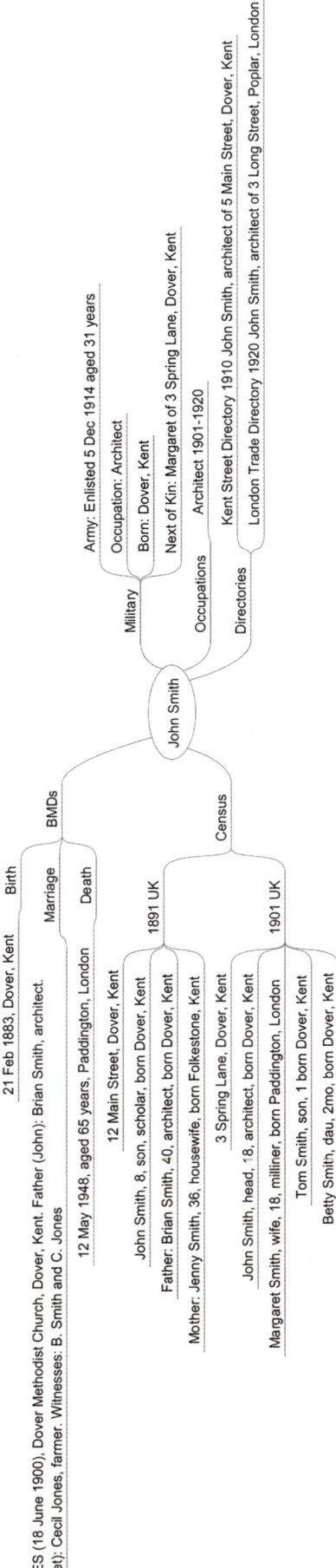

Freemind Map

	Price	Availability	Access	Website
Freemind	Free	Windows, MacOS and Linux (Need Java)	Download software	www.freemind.sourceforge.net

Freemind Grid

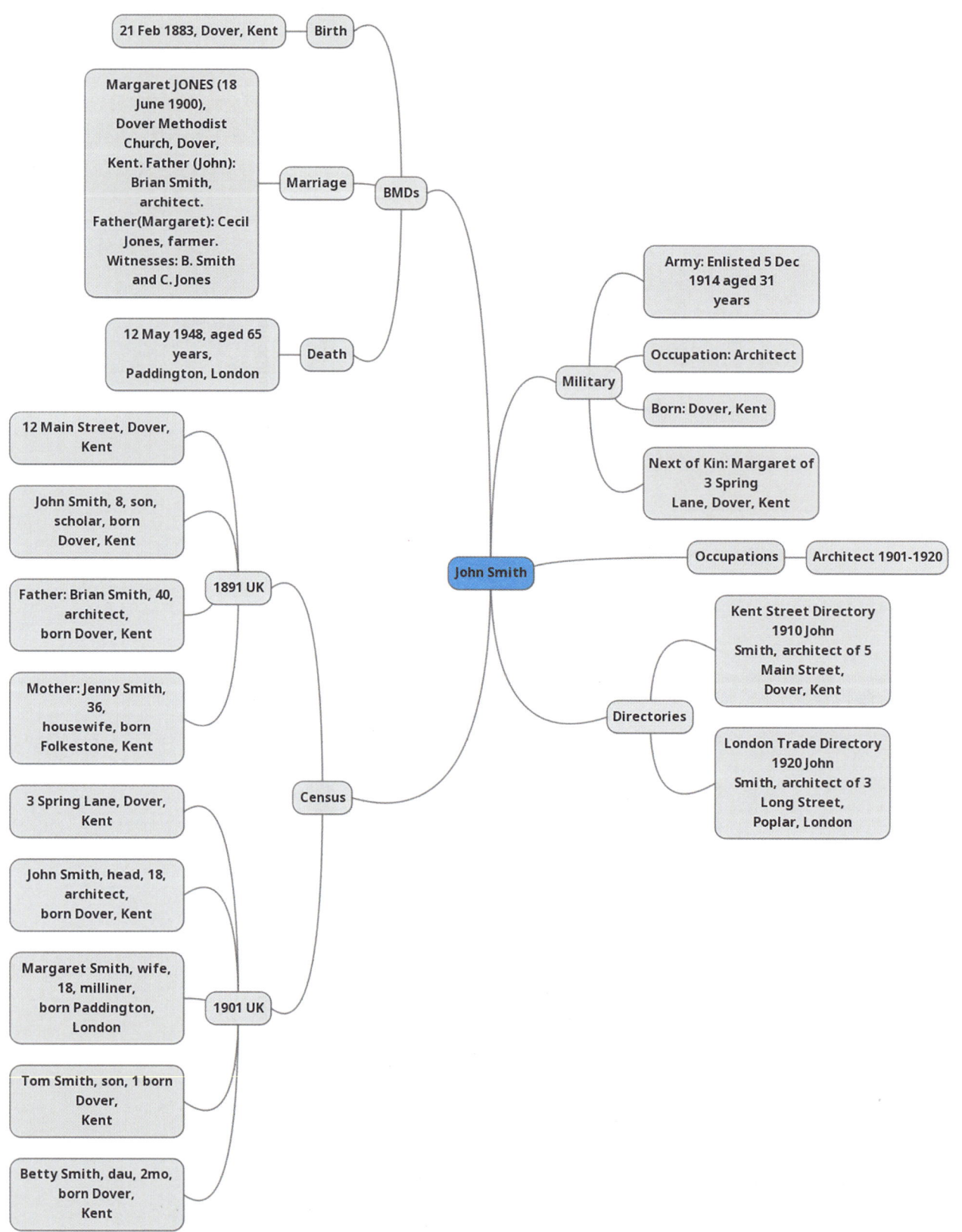

MindMup Map

	Price	Availability	Access	Website
MindMup	Free (Limited space) Paid (Unlimited use)	Windows, MacOS and Linux	Online and web-based	www.mindmup.com/

MindMup Grid

MIND-MAPPING MADE EASY FOR FAMILY HISTORIANS

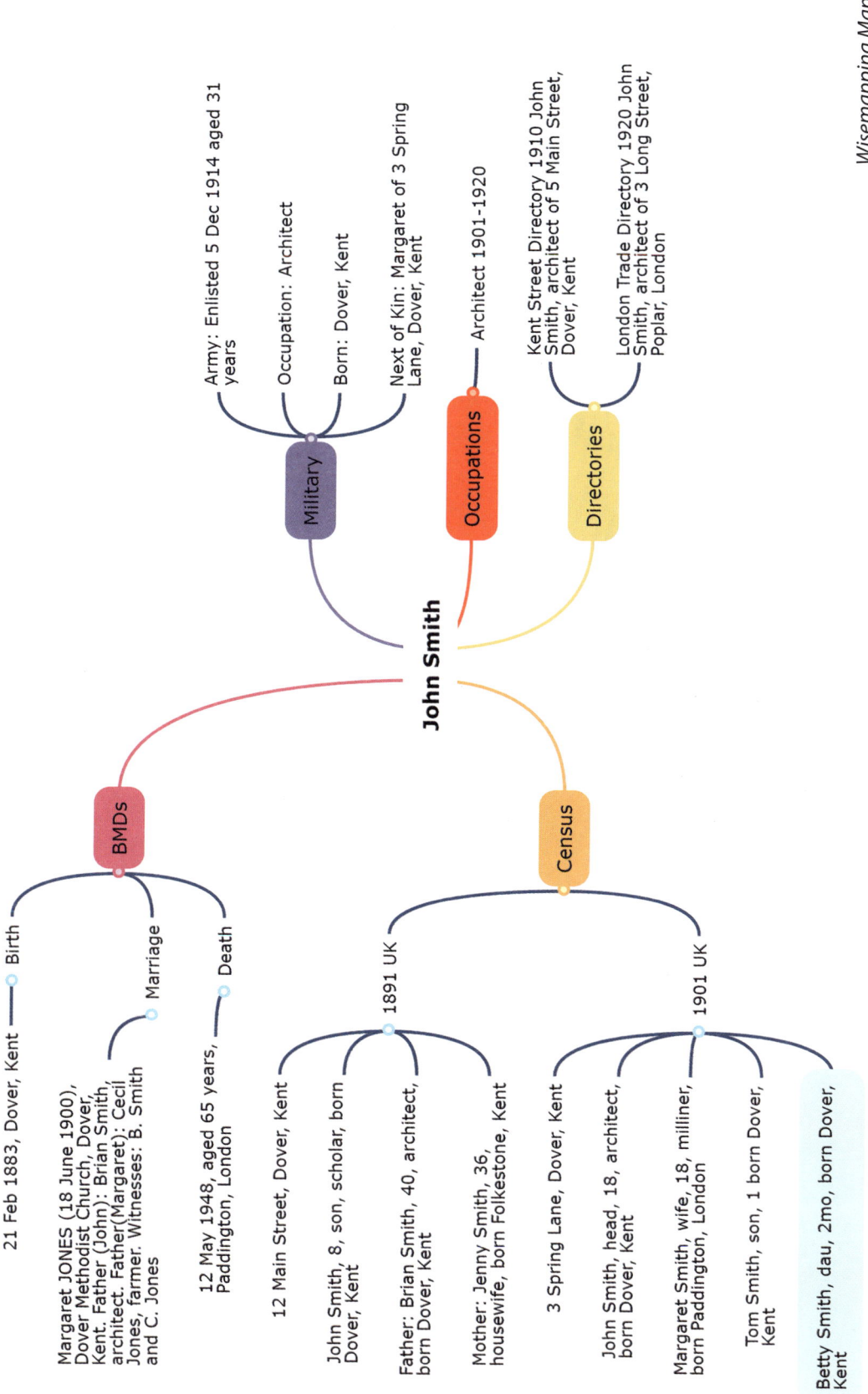

Wisemapping Map

Price	Availability	Access	Website
WiseMapping	Free	Web application	Download software	www.wisemapping.com/

Wisemapping Grid

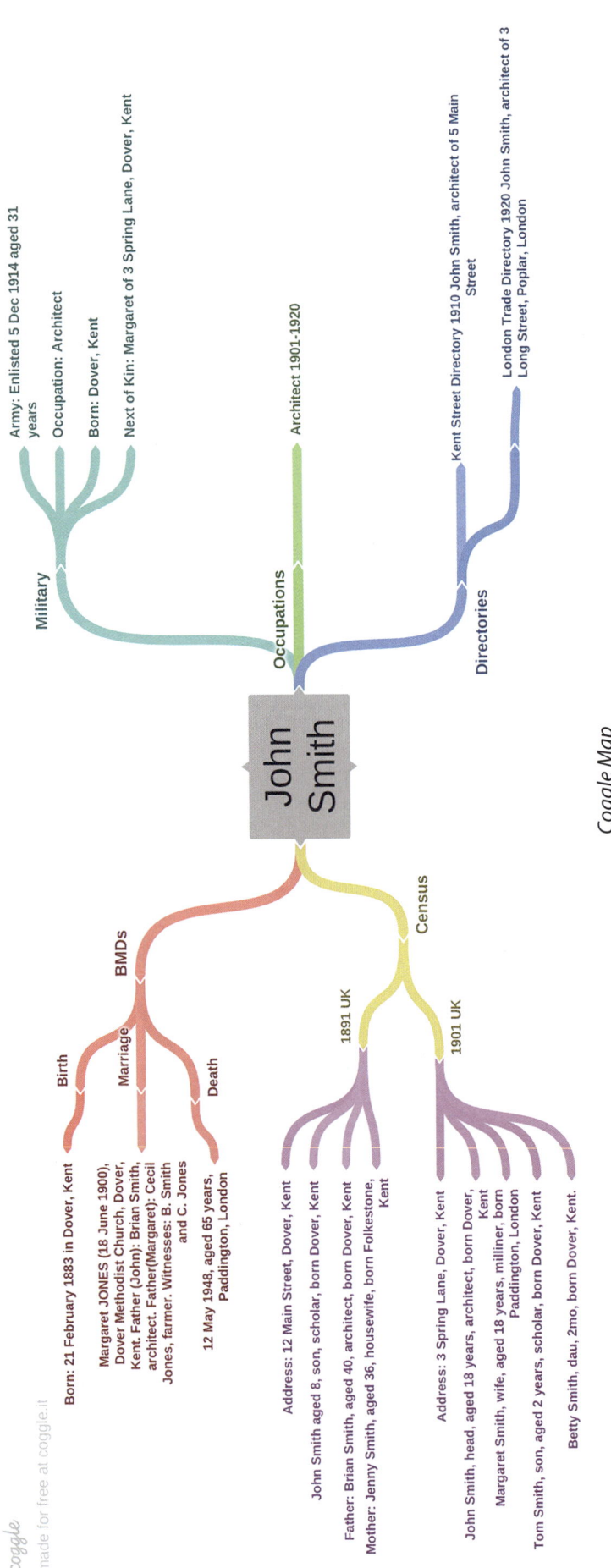

Coggle Map

	Price	Availability	Access	Website
Coggle	Free (Limited space) Paid (Unlimited use)	Web application	Online and web-based	www.coggle.it/

Coggle Grid

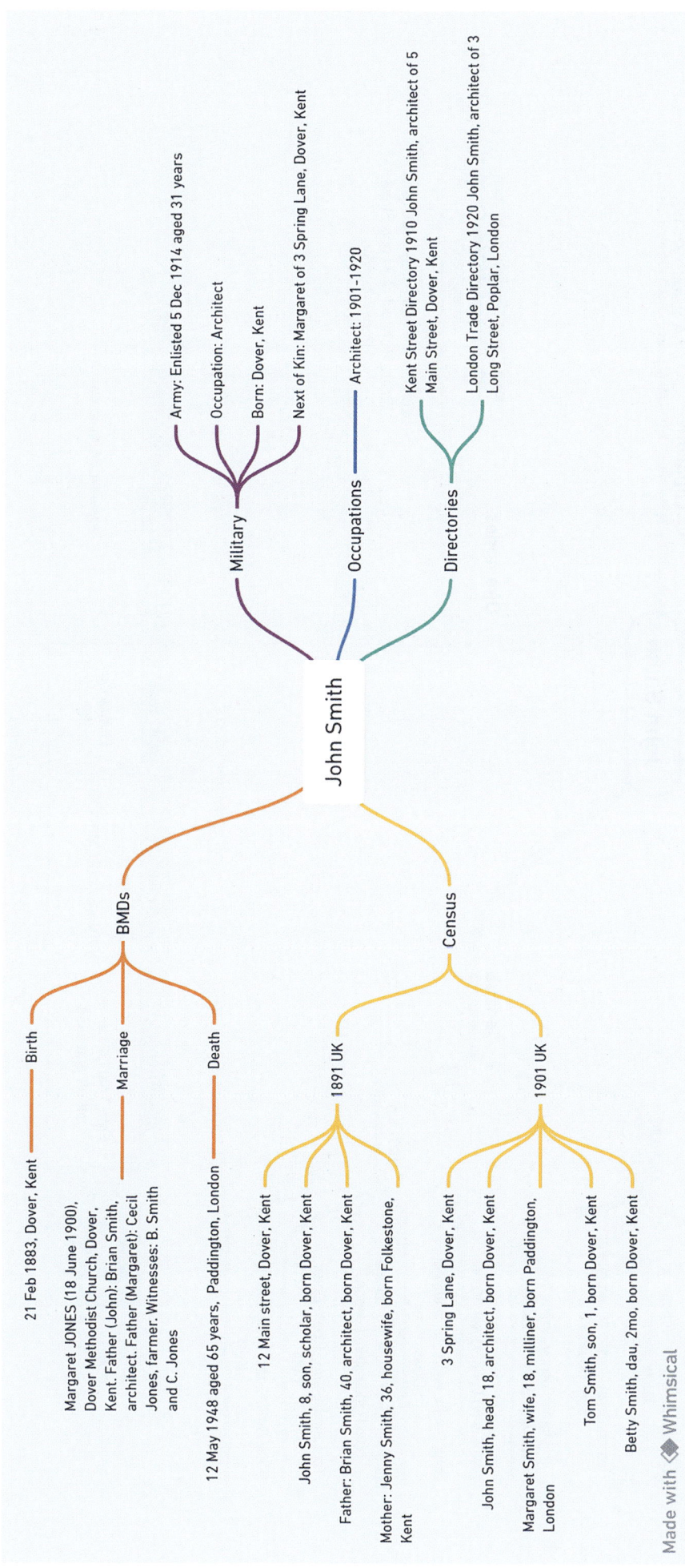

Whimsical Map

	Price	Availability	Access	Website
Whimsical	Free (Limited space) Paid (Unlimited use)	Web application and Desktop application	Online and web-based	www.whimsical.com

Whimsical Grid

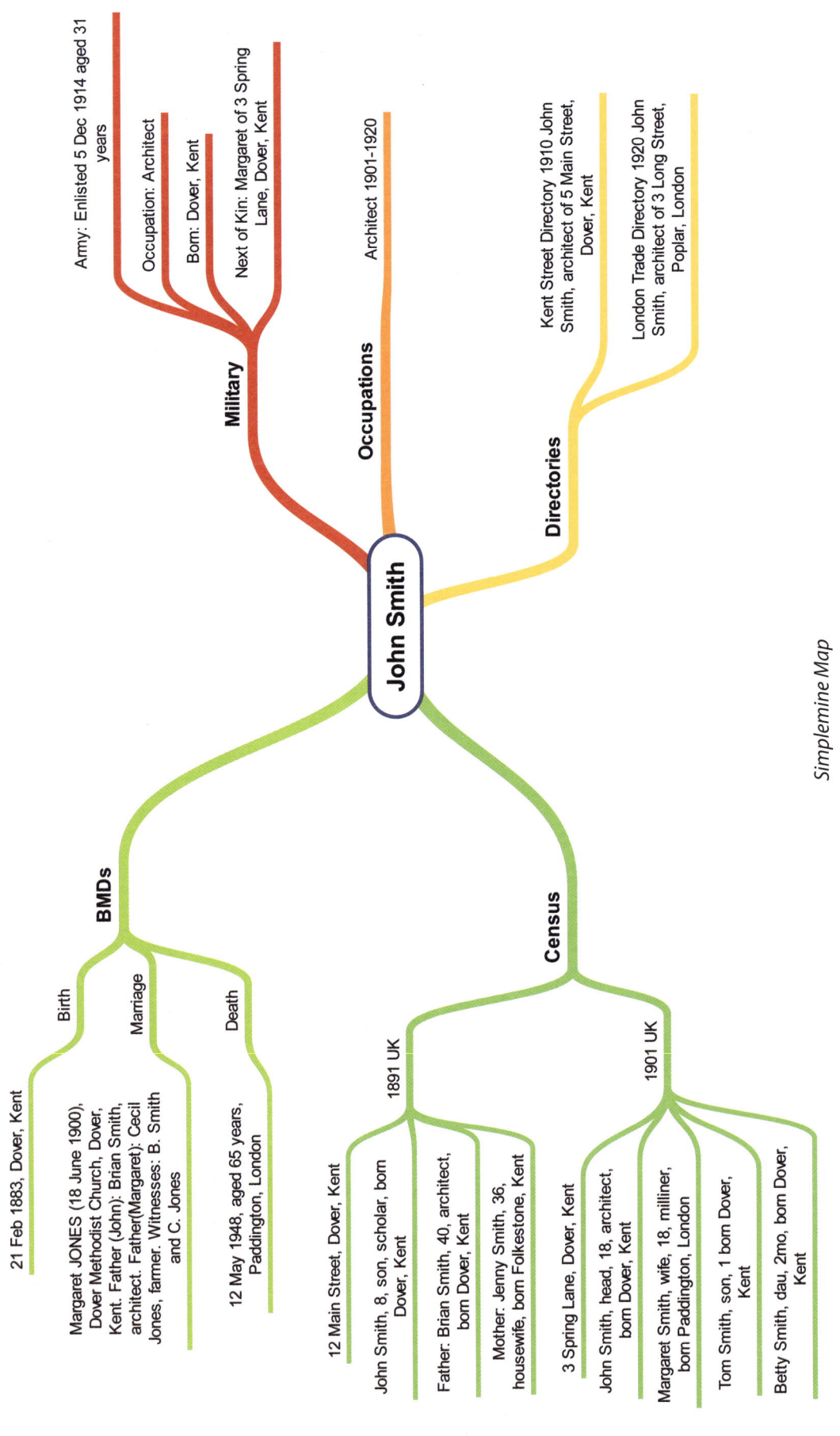

Simplemine Map

	Price	Availability	Access	Website
SimpleMind	Free Trial (30 days) One off purchase	Windows and MacOS.	Download software	www.simplemind.eu

Simplemind Grid

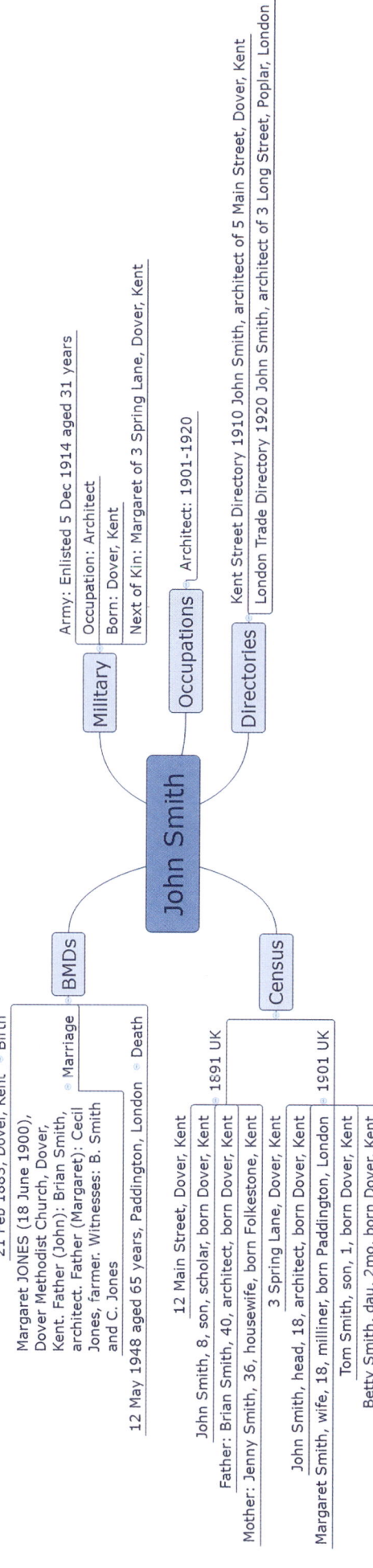

XMind Map

	Price	Availability	Access	Website
Xmind	Free Trial One off purchase	Windows, MacOS and Linux	Download software	www.xmind.net/

XMind Grid

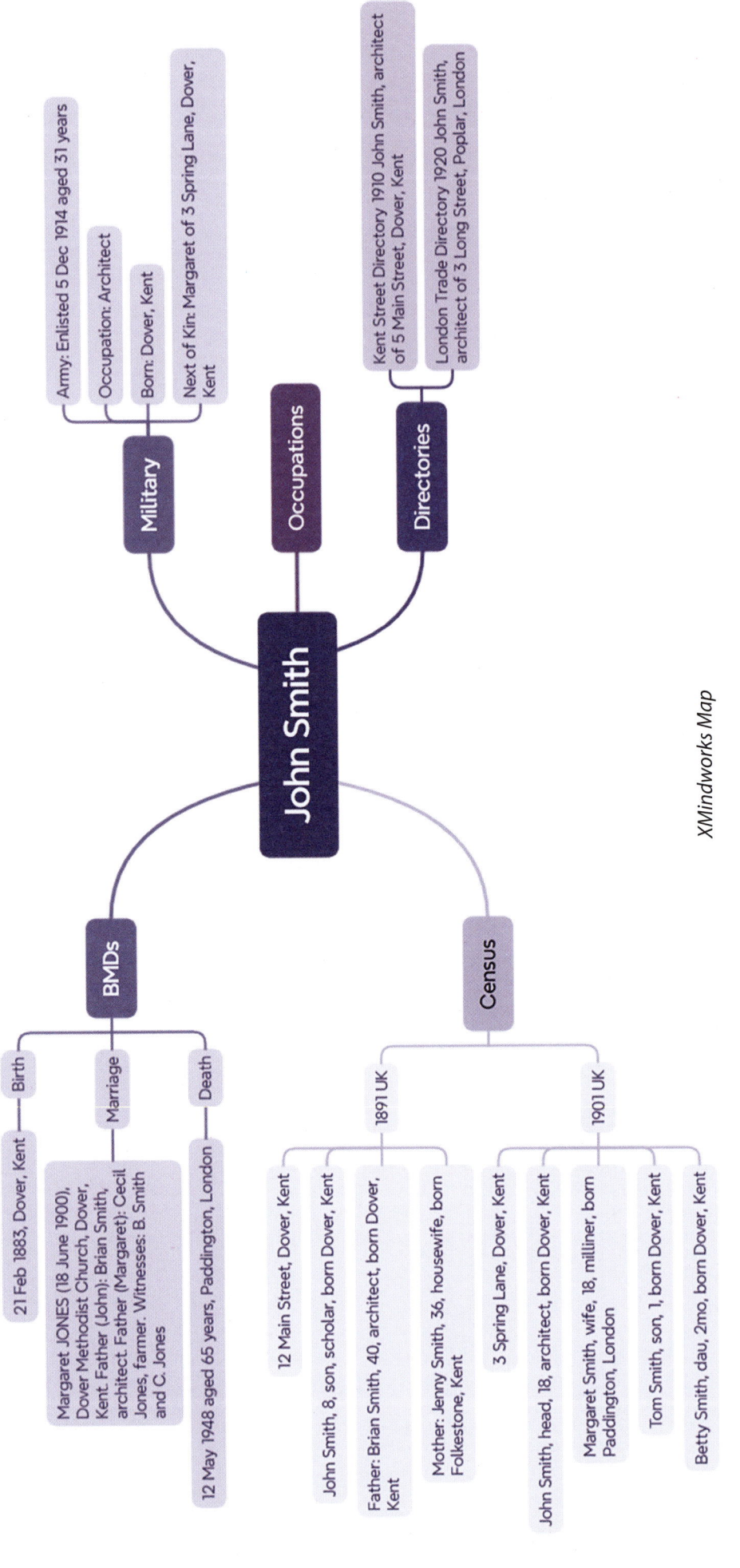

XMindworks Map

Price	Availability	Access	Website
Free (Some limitations) Paid (Unlimited use)	Web application	Online and web-based	www.xmind.works
Xmind.works			

XMindworks Grid

MIND-MAPPING MADE EASY FOR FAMILY HISTORIANS

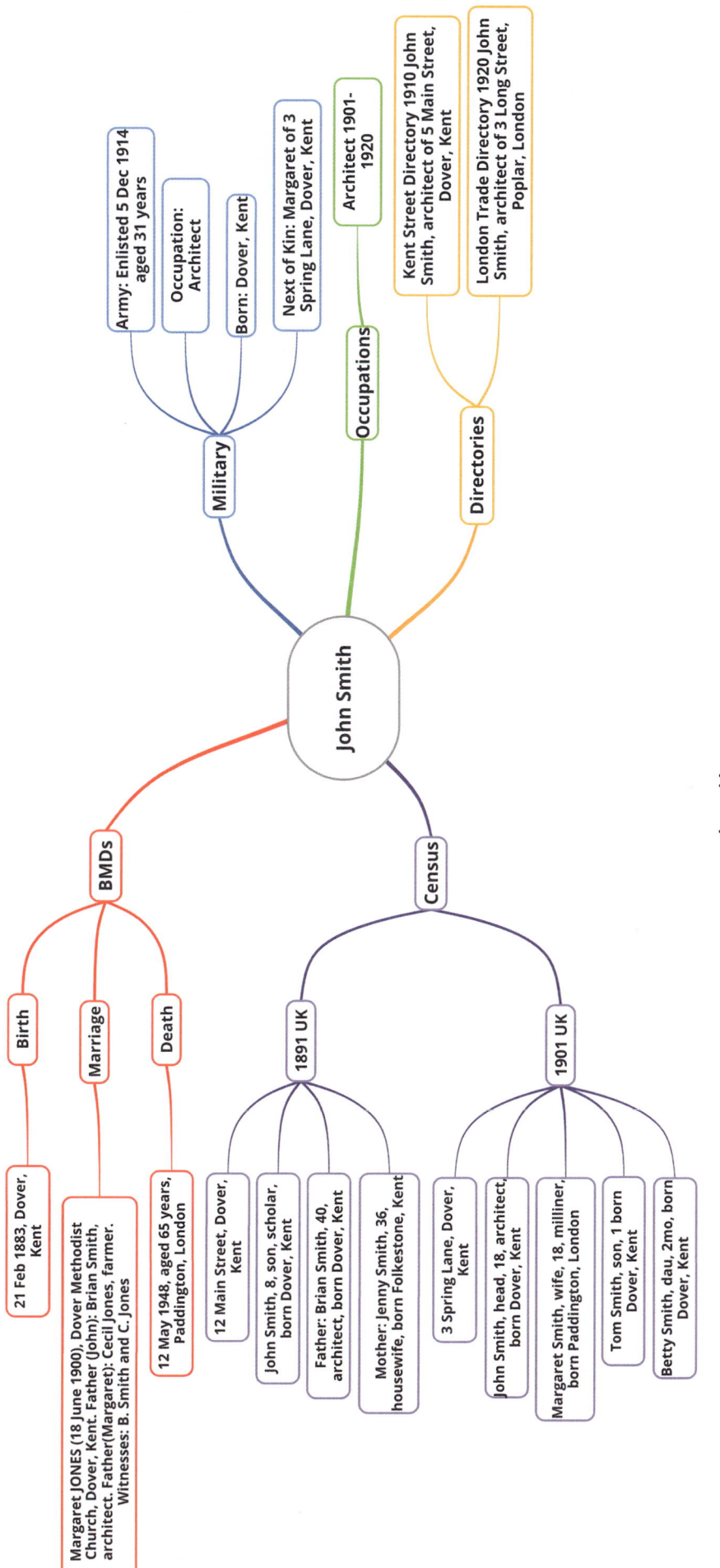

Ayoa Map

Price	Availability	Access	Website
Free (Design limitations) Paid (Unlimited use)			
Ayoa	Web application	Online and web-based	www.ayoa.com

Ayoa Grid

67

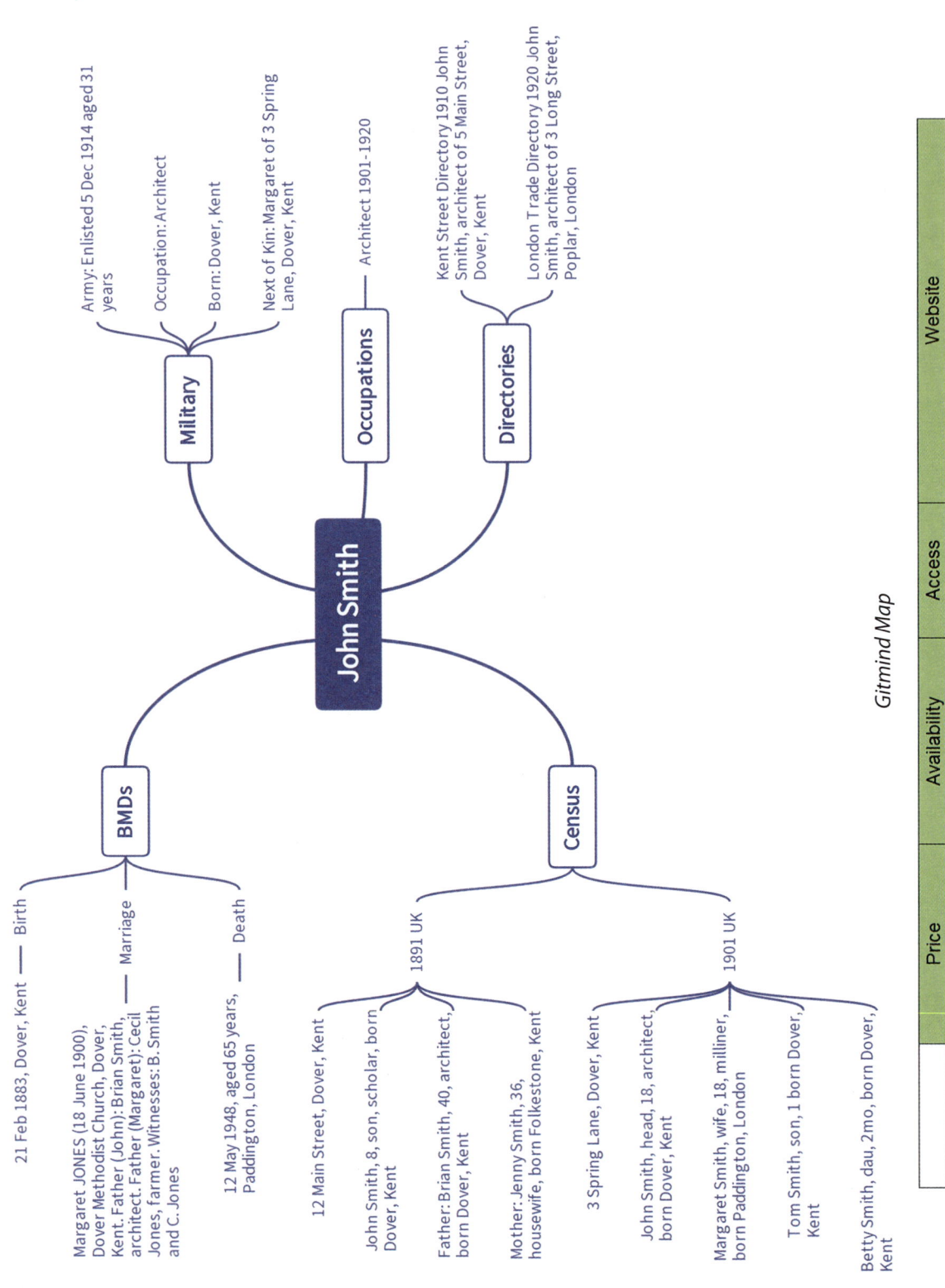

Gitmind Map

Price	Availability	Access	Website
Free (limited space) Paid (Unlimited use)	Windows and MacOS. Mobile versions for Android and IOS	Download software	www.gitmind.com
Gitmind			

Gitmind Grid

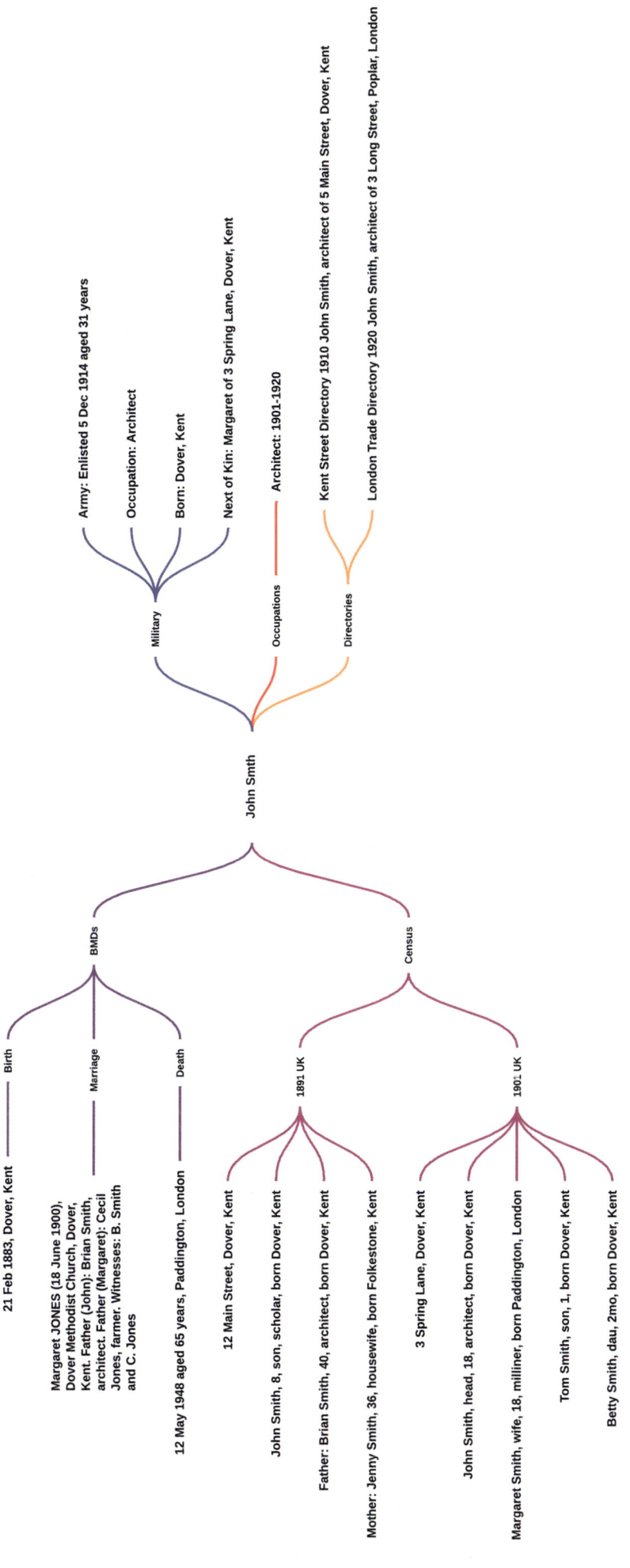

LucidChart Map

	Price	Availability	Access	Website
LucidChart	Free (Limited space) Paid (Unlimited use)	Web application	Online and web-based	www.lucidchart.com

LucidChart Grid

69

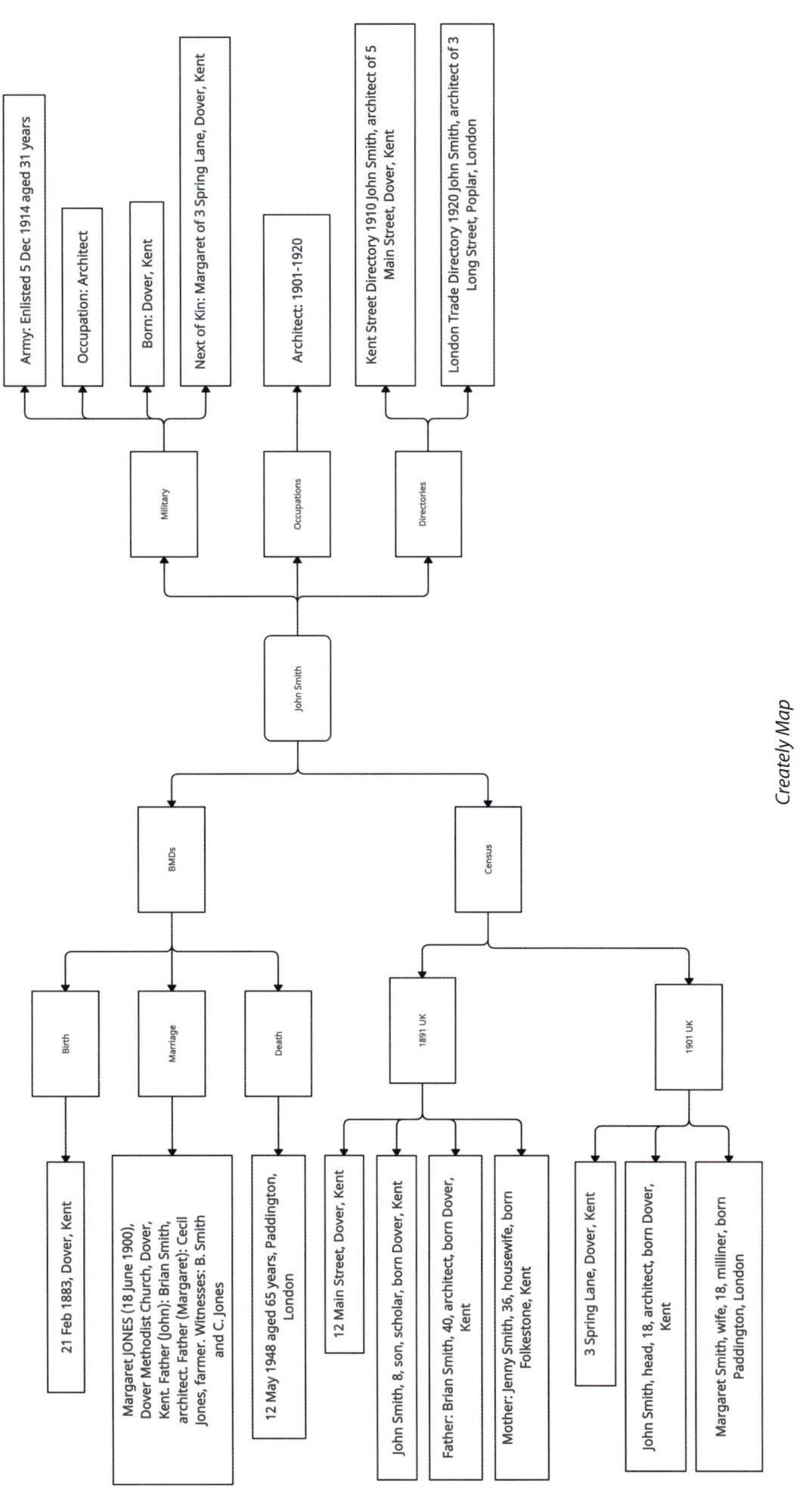

Creately Map

	Price	Availability	Access	Website
Creately	Free (Limited space) Paid (Unlimited use)	Web application	Online and web-based	www.creately.com

Creately Grid

MIND-MAPPING MADE EASY FOR FAMILY HISTORIANS

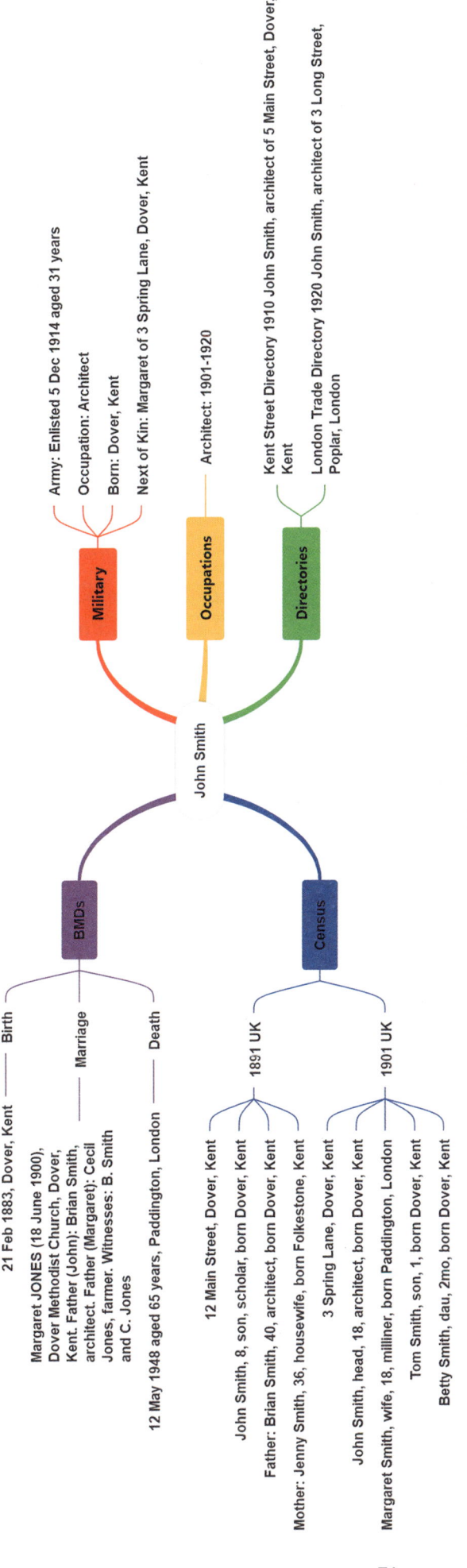

EdrawMind Map

	Price	Availability	Access	Website
EdrawMind	Free (Limited space and export with watermark)) Paid (Unlimited use)	Windows, MacOS and Linux, and mobile versions for Android and IOS	Download software	www.edrawsoft.com

EdrawMind Grid

CONCLUSION

Having reached the end of our mind-mapping journey together, I hope that your interest has been piqued enough and you will give it a go! Seriously, mind maps are like the superheroes of the genealogy world – easy to use and incredibly handy.

Mind maps are remarkably adaptable. Whether you are digging into dusty records, uncovering the secrets of your house, planning an exciting research trip, or tackling a tricky genealogy puzzle, mind maps are your trusty companions every step of the way.

The real strength of mind maps lies in their flexibility. They handle both structured and unstructured data, providing a practical means to validate or challenge connections within your family history.

Mind maps truly are an excellent asset and they deserve a place in every genealogist's toolbox. In the maze of family history, let mind maps be your guides, untangling the web of information and propelling your research forward. Trust me, your family tree and research techniques are about to undergo a serious makeover – mind-map style! And you never know … you may even come to wonder how on earth you managed without them!

LIST OF ILLUSTRATIONS

John Smith mind map 3
The eight parts of speech table. 4
The eight parts of speech mind map. 5
Planning your research – Plympton St Mary Workhouse mind map. 23
Analysing a person – Johann Schaffert mind map 25
Identifying gaps in your research – Joseph Richardson mind map 27
1862 Removal order for John Dunn 28
Analysing a document – removal order mind map 29
Planning a research trip mind map 31
Constructing a village study mind map 33
Carrying out a house history mind map. 36–37
Mindmeister map. 58
Mindmeister grid 58
Freemind map. 59
Freemind grid 59
MindMup map 60
MindMup grid 60
Wisemapping map 61
Wisemapping grid 61
Coggle map 62
Coggle grid. 62
Whimsical map 63
Whimsical grid. 63
Simplemind map 64
Simplemind grid. 64
XMind map. 65
XMind grid 65
XMindworks map. 66
XMindworks grid 66
Ayoa map 67
Ayoa grid 67
Gitmind map 68
Gitmind grid. 68
LucidChart map 69
LucidChart grid. 69
Creately map 70
Creately grid. 70
EdrawMind map 71
EdrawMind grid 71

BIBLIOGRAPHY AND FURTHER READING

Buzan, Tony and Dominic O'Brien, *Mind Map Mastery: The Complete Guide to Learning and Using the Most Powerful Thinking Tool in the Universe* (Watkins, an imprint of Watkins Media Limited London 2018)

Knight, Kam, *Mind Mapping: Improve Memory, Concentration, Communication, Organization, Creativity, and Time Management* (CreateSpace Independent Publishing Platform 2012)

Medina, John, *Brain Rules* (Pear Press 2014)

Rustler, Florian, *Mind Mapping for Dummies* (Wiley 2012)

Wisdom University, *The Secrets Behind Mind Mapping: Top Tier Tips On Idea Mapping That Can Help You Ace Any Task* (Independently 2023)

USEFUL GENEALOGY WEBSITES

Ancestry	www.ancestry.co.uk
FamilySearch	www.familysearch.org
FindMyPast	www.findmypast.com
FreeBMD	www.freebmd.org.uk
FreeREG	www.freereg.org.uk
General Register Office	www.gro.gov.uk
GENUKI	www.genuki.org.uk
The National Archives	www.nationalarchives.gov.uk
The Genealogist	www.thegenealogist.co.uk
UK BMD	www.ukbmd.org.uk

MIND-MAPPING SOFTWARE WEBSITES

Ayoa	www.ayoa.com
Coggle	www.coggle.it
Creately	www.creately.com
EdrawMind	www.edrawsoft.com
Freemind	www.freemind.sourceforge.net
Gitmind	www.gitmind.com
LucidChart	www.lucidchart.com
Mindmeister	www.mindmeister.com
MindMup	www.mindmup.com
Simplemind	www.simplemind.eu
Whimsical	www.whimsical.com
Wisemapping	www.wisemapping.com
XMind	www.xmind.net
XMindworks	www.xmind.works